BBC goodfood

QUICK & HEALTHY

Editor **Tracey Raye**

BOOKS

BBC Books, an imprint of Ebury Publishing
20 Vauxhall Bridge Road,
London SW1V 2SA

BBC Books is part of the Penguin Random House group of companies whose addresses can be found at
global.penguinrandomhouse.com

Penguin
Random House
UK

All recipes contained in this book first appeared in *BBC Good Food magazine*.

First published by BBC Books in 2022

www.penguin.co.uk

A CIP catalogue record for this book is available from the British Library

ISBN 9781785947889

Printed and bound in Latvia by Livonia Print

Project Editors: Nell Warner and Kay Halsey
Design: Interstate Creative Partners Ltd and Peppis Designworks
Cover Design: Two Associates
Production: Catherine Ngwong
Picture Researcher: Gabby Harrington

MIX
Paper from
responsible sources
FSC® C018179
www.fsc.org

PICTURE AND RECIPE CREDITS

BBC Books would like to thank the following people for providing photos. While every effort has been made to trace and
acknowledge all photographers, we should like to apologise should there be any errors or omissions.

Will Heap p11, p31, p41, p45, p141, p157; David Munns p13, p63, p91, p95, p121; Lis Parsons p15, p51, p75, p119, p123, p125, p127,
p129; Roger Stowell p17; Melissa Reynolds-James p19, p59, p79; Mike English p21, p87, p105, p163, p165, p167, p175, p177, p181,
p193, p195, p197, p199, p201, p203, p211; Jon Whitaker p23; Rob Streeter p27, p135, p145, p159, p169, p209; Faith Mason p29,
p61; Philip Webb p33, p35; Steve Baxter p37; Gareth Morgans p39, p73, p113, p151, p185; Jonathan Kennedy p43; Sam Stowell
p47, p97, p99, p111, p117; Sian Irvine p49; Stuart Ovenden p65, p69, p100, p103, p137, p139, p153, p161, p205; Howard Shooter
p71; Simon Walton p83; Louise Hagger p93; Myles New p107, p147; Peter Cassidy p109, p171, p187, p207; David Loftus p143;
Clare Winfield p173; Amanda Heywood p179; Emma Boyns p183

All the recipes in this book were created by the editorial team at *Good Food* and by regular contributors to BBC Magazines.

Contents

Introduction

Following a healthy diet can seem like a tricky task, especially when you're managing a busy schedule at the same time. That's why we've pulled together this collection of quick and healthy recipes that are just perfect for those times when you need a balanced and healthy meal in minutes. We believe that good health starts with good food and a diet that is delicious, accessible and balanced in all the essential nutrients required to help you look and feel your best.

You'll notice that the following recipes include plenty of fruits, veg, lean proteins and healthy fats, while minimising ultra-processed foods. All the recipes in this book can be prepared in 30 minutes or less and provide four servings. You'll also discover a variety of vegan and vegetarian recipes for those who are interested in including healthier plant-based dishes in their diet.

Each recipe has been analysed on a per-serving basis by a registered nutritionist, so you can see exactly what each dish contains. To qualify for our healthy tag, all the recipes selected in this book contain no more than 5g saturated fat, 15g sugar and 1.5g salt. They've also been checked to ensure that they have low-to-medium levels of fat, saturated fat, sugar and salt per 100g. Please note: ingredients listed as serving suggestions are not included in the nutritional analysis.

We hope that these recipes will serve to inspire and support a healthier, happier you.

Tracey Raye
Health editor, *BBC Good Food*

Notes & conversion tables

NOTES ON THE RECIPES
- Eggs are large in the UK and Australia and extra large in America unless stated.
- Wash fresh produce before preparation.
- Recipes contain nutritional analyses for 'sugars', which means the total sugar content including all natural sugars in the ingredients, unless otherwise stated.

OVEN TEMPERATURES

GAS	°C	°C FAN	°F	OVEN TEMP.
¼	110	90	225	Very cool
½	120	100	250	Very cool
1	140	120	275	Cool or slow
2	150	130	300	Cool or slow
3	160	140	325	Warm
4	180	160	350	Moderate
5	190	170	375	Moderately hot
6	200	180	400	Fairly hot
7	220	200	425	Hot
8	230	210	450	Very hot
9	240	220	475	Very hot

APPROXIMATE WEIGHT CONVERSIONS
Cup measurements, which are used in Australia and America, have not been listed here as they vary from ingredient to ingredient. Kitchen scales should be used to measure dry/solid ingredients.

Good Food cares about sustainable sourcing and animal welfare. Where possible, humanely reared meats, sustainably caught fish (see fishonline.org for further information from the Marine Conservation Society) and free-range chickens and eggs are used when recipes are originally tested.

SPOON MEASURES

Spoon measurements are level unless otherwise specified.

- 1 teaspoon (tsp) = 5ml
- 1 tablespoon (tbsp) = 15ml
- 1 Australian tablespoon = 20ml (cooks in Australia should measure 3 teaspoons where 1 tablespoon is specified in a recipe)

APPROXIMATE LIQUID CONVERSIONS

METRIC	IMPERIAL	AUS	US
50ml	2fl oz	¼ cup	¼ cup
125ml	4fl oz	½ cup	½ cup
175ml	6fl oz	¾ cup	¾ cup
225ml	8fl oz	1 cup	1 cup
300ml	10fl oz/½ pint	½ pint	1¼ cups
450ml	16fl oz	2 cups	2 cups/1 pint
600ml	20fl oz/1 pint	1 pint	2½ cups
1 litre	35fl oz/1¾ pints	1¾ pints	1 quart

Chapter 1

POULTRY

· ·

Poultry is such a versatile meat that can be used in a variety of dishes. Here you'll discover recipes for curries, pastas and warming stews. Meats such as chicken and turkey offer a brilliant source of lean protein, B vitamins and minerals, such as zinc, magnesium and selenium. Even better, they cook in minutes, making them a great choice for speedy suppers.

Chicken & veg bowl

Make this colourful chicken, brown rice and vegetable dish for the whole family. With avocado, edamame beans, sweetcorn and carrots, it's healthy and tasty.

 PREP 15 mins COOK 15 mins  SERVES 4

- 250g brown basmati rice
- 1 tbsp rapeseed oil
- 1 garlic clove, crushed
- 2 chicken breasts, sliced
- 2 tbsp hoisin sauce
- 100g frozen edamame beans or peas, defrosted
- 100g frozen sweetcorn
- 100g carrots, grated
- 100g red peppers, cut into small cubes
- 1 avocado, stoned and sliced
- 1 lemon, cut into quarters, to serve (optional)

1 Cook the rice following pack instructions, then drain and return to the pan to keep warm. Heat the oil in a frying pan or wok, add the garlic and fry for 2 mins or until golden. Tip in the chicken and fry until the pieces are cooked through, then stir in the hoisin sauce, season and continue cooking for a further 2 mins. Cook the edamame beans and sweetcorn in simmering water for 2 mins, then drain.

2 Divide the rice between four bowls and top with the chicken slices in a strip down the middle, with the carrot, red pepper, beans or peas, sweetcorn and avocado down either side. Serve with the lemon to squeeze over, if you like.

Nutrition per serving
energy 460 kcals, fat 13g, saturates 2g, carbs 54g, sugars 7g, fibre 7g, protein 1g, salt 0.4g

Oven-baked chicken pilau

This chicken pilau is not only satisfying, it's healthy too.

 PREP 5 mins COOK 25 mins SERVES 4

- 85g pine nuts
- 2 tbsp olive oil
- 1 red onion, cut into thin wedges
- 1 tsp turmeric
- 8 skinless boneless chicken thighs
- 350g long grain rice
- 70g sultanas
- 850ml chicken stock
- handful coriander leaves, to serve

1 Heat the oven to 200C/fan 180C/gas 6. On the hob, toast the pine nuts in a flameproof casserole dish, remove and set aside.

2 Heat the oil in the casserole and soften the onion with the turmeric for 3 mins. Add the chicken thighs and cook for 3–4 mins until browned all over. Tip in the rice, sultanas and 700ml stock, then bring to the boil. Cover with a lid and bake in the oven for 20 mins, checking halfway and adding more stock if needed. Cook until the chicken is done and the rice tender. Season to taste, then stir in the toasted pine nuts and serve sprinkled with fresh coriander.

Nutrition per serving
energy 774 kcals, fat 29g, saturates 4g, carbs 86g, sugars 15g, fibre 4g, protein 39g, salt 1.34g

Chicken & apricot stew

Stay on track with this low-fat supper that's on the table in half an hour.

 PREP 10 mins COOK 20 mins  SERVES 4

- 1 tbsp olive oil
- 1 onion, chopped
- 1 garlic clove, crushed
- 1 tbsp ras-el-hanout or Moroccan spice mix
- 4 skinless chicken breasts, sliced
- 300ml reduced-salt chicken stock
- 400g can chickpeas, drained
- 12 dried apricots, sliced
- small bunch coriander, chopped

1 Heat the oil in a large shallow pan, then cook the onion for 3 mins. Add the garlic and spices and cook for a further min. Tip in the chicken and cook for 3 mins, then pour in the chicken stock, chickpeas and apricots. Simmer for 5 mins or until the chicken is cooked through. Stir through the coriander and serve immediately with couscous and a green salad, if you like.

Nutrition per serving
energy 309 kcals, fat 6g, saturates 1g, carbs 24g, sugars 13g, fibre 5g, protein 40g, salt 0.66g

15-minute chicken pasta

Enjoy fast food with a mouthwateringly healthy chicken pasta – low in fat too.

 PREP 5 min COOK 10 mins  SERVES 4

- 350g pasta bows (farfalle)
- 300g broccoli, cut into small florets
- 1 tbsp olive oil
- 3 large skinless chicken breasts, cut into bite-sized chunks
- 2 garlic cloves, crushed
- 2 tbsp wholegrain mustard
- juice 1 large or 2 small oranges
- 25g flaked almonds, toasted

1 Cook the pasta in plenty of boiling salted water according to the packet instructions. Three minutes before the pasta is cooked, throw the broccoli into the pasta water and continue to boil.

2 While the pasta is cooking, gently heat the oil in a large frying pan or wok. Tip in the chicken and fry, stirring occasionally, until the chicken pieces are cooked and golden, about 8–10 minutes, adding the garlic for the last 2 minutes.

3 Mix the mustard with the orange juice in a small bowl. Pour the mixture over the chicken, and gently simmer for a minute or two. Drain the pasta and broccoli, reserving 3 tablespoons of the pasta water. Toss the pasta and broccoli with the chicken, stir in the pasta water and the almonds, season well and serve.

Nutrition per serving
energy 531 kcals, fat 11g, saturates 1g, carbs 70g, sugars 0g, fibre 6g, protein 43g, salt 0.52g

Chicken with crushed harissa chickpeas

Need something speedy for dinner? Try this chicken, coated in flavourful za'atar and served with spiced chickpeas. It's simple, but seriously delicious.

 PREP 5 mins COOK 10 mins  SERVES 4

- 2 tbsp rapeseed oil
- 1 onion, chopped
- 1 red pepper, finely sliced
- 1 yellow pepper, finely sliced
- 4 skinless chicken breasts
- 1 tbsp za'atar
- 400g can chickpeas
- 1½ tbsp red harissa paste
- 150g baby spinach
- ½ small bunch parsley, finely chopped
- lemon wedges, to serve

1 Heat 1 tbsp of oil in a frying pan over a medium heat and fry the onion and peppers for 7 mins until softened and golden.

2 Meanwhile, put the chicken between two sheets of baking parchment and lightly bash until about 2cm thick. Mix the remaining oil and the za'atar together, then rub over the chicken. Season to taste.

3 Heat the grill to high. Put the chicken on a baking tray lined with foil, and grill for 3–4 mins each side, or until golden and cooked through.

4 Heat the chickpeas in a pan with the harissa paste and 2 tbsp water until warmed through, then roughly mash with a potato masher. Wilt the spinach in a pan with 1 tbsp of water or in the microwave in a heatproof bowl. Stir the pepper and onion mixture, spinach and parsley through the chickpeas. Serve with the sliced chicken and the lemon wedges for squeezing over.

Nutrition per serving
energy 366 kcals, fat 12g, saturates 2g, carbs 16g, sugars 6g, fibre 7g, protein 44g, salt 0.6g

Fridge-raid fried rice

Pack in the veg with this healthy chicken fried rice, which uses everyday foods you'll find in the fridge for a quick and easy family supper.

 PREP 15 mins COOK 15 mins  SERVES 4

- 2 tbsp vegetable oil
- 1 white onion, finely chopped
- 1 carrot, finely chopped
- 100g green beans, chopped
- 1 red or yellow pepper, finely chopped
- ½ medium broccoli, chopped into small florets
- 150g cooked chicken (or any other meat), roughly chopped
- 300g cold cooked rice
- 2 eggs, beaten
- 1 tbsp sesame oil
- 1 tbsp oyster sauce
- 1 spring onion, finely sliced
- 1 tsp toasted sesame seeds

1 Heat half the vegetable oil in a wok or a frying pan over a medium-high heat, and stir-fry the onion, carrot and green beans for 5 mins. Add the peppers, broccoli and chicken, and stir-fry for 3 mins more.

2 Tip in the rice and stir-fry for another 4 mins until all the grains of rice have separated. Push the rice and vegetables to the side, then add the remaining vegetable oil to the other. Crack in the egg and scramble briefly before stirring into the veg and chicken mixture.

3 Stir in the sesame oil and oyster sauce to coat, then garnish with the spring onions and sesame seeds.

Nutrition per serving
energy 388 kcals, fat 20g, saturates 3g, carbs 29g, sugars 7g, fibre 7g, protein 20g, salt 0.6g

One-pot harissa chicken

This hearty chicken casserole is low in fat, packed with veg and flavoured with harissa for a satisfying supper.

PREP 5 mins COOK 25 mins   SERVES 4

- 4 skinless chicken breasts
- 1 tsp ground cumin
- 1 tbsp olive oil
- 1 onion, finely sliced
- 400g can cherry tomatoes
- 2 tbsp harissa paste
- 1 tbsp clear honey
- 2 courgettes, thickly sliced
- 400g can chickpeas, drained and rinsed

1 Season the chicken breasts all over with the cumin and lots of ground black pepper. Heat the oil in a large non-stick frying pan and cook the chicken with the onion for 4 mins. Turn the chicken over and cook for a further 3 mins. Stir the onions around the chicken regularly as they cook.

2 Tip the tomatoes and 250ml water into the pan and stir in the harissa, honey, courgettes and chickpeas. Bring to a gentle simmer and cook for 15 mins until the chicken is tender and the sauce has thickened slightly.

Nutrition per serving
energy 293 kcals, fat 6g, saturates 1g, carbs 22g, sugars 10g, fibre 4g, protein 36g, salt 0.9g

Lemon-spiced chicken with chickpeas

A spicy, filling one pot that has a bit of added zing and offers 2 of your 5-a-day. Make it a midweek must.

 PREP 5 mins COOK 15 mins  SERVES 4

- 1 tbsp sunflower oil
- 1 onion, halved and thinly sliced
- 4 skinless chicken breasts, cut into chunks
- 1 cinnamon stick, broken in half
- 1 tsp ground coriander
- 1 tsp ground cumin
- zest and juice 1 lemon
- 400g can chickpeas, drained
- 200ml chicken stock
- 250g bag spinach

1 Heat the oil in a large frying pan, then fry the onion gently for 5 mins. Turn up the heat and add the chicken, frying for about 3 mins until golden brown.

2 Stir in the spices and lemon zest, fry for 1 more min, then tip in the chickpeas and stock. Put the lid on and simmer for 5 mins.

3 Season to taste, then tip in spinach and re-cover. Leave to wilt for 2 mins, then stir through. Squeeze over the lemon juice just before serving.

Nutrition per serving
energy 290 kcals, fat 7g, saturates 1g, carbs 14g, sugars 3g, fibre 4g, protein 42g, salt 1.03g

Pomegranate chicken with couscous

Jazz up chicken breasts in this fruity, sweetly spiced sauce with pomegranate seeds, toasted almonds and tagine paste.

 PREP 5 mins COOK 15 mins   SERVES 4

- 1 tbsp vegetable oil
- 200g couscous
- 1 chicken stock cube
- 1 large red onion, halved and thinly sliced
- 600g chicken mini fillets
- 4 tbsp tagine spice paste or 2 tbsp harissa paste
- 190ml bottle pomegranate juice (not sweetened)
- 100g pack pomegranate seeds
- 100g pack toasted flaked almonds
- small pack mint, chopped

1 Boil the kettle and heat the oil in a large frying pan. Put the couscous in a bowl with some seasoning and crumble in half the stock cube. Add the onion to the pan and fry for a few mins to soften. Pour boiling water over the couscous to just cover, then cover the bowl with a tea towel and set aside.

2 Push the onion to one side of the pan, add the chicken fillets and brown on all sides. Stir in the tagine paste or harissa and the pomegranate juice, then crumble in the rest of the stock cube and season well. Simmer, uncovered, for 10 mins until the sauce has thickened and the chicken is cooked through. Stir through the pomegranate seeds, saving a few to scatter over before serving.

3 After 5 mins, fluff up the couscous with a fork and stir through the almonds and mint. Serve the chicken on the couscous with the sauce spooned over.

Nutrition per serving
energy 590 kcals, fat 20g, saturates 2g, carbs 50g, sugars 14g, fibre 4g, protein 50g, salt 0.4g

Jerk-seasoned chicken pilaf

Make this jerk-seasoned chicken pilaf for an easy midweek meal. It takes 30 minutes from prep to plate, so makes a speedy, as well as healthy, supper.

 PREP 10 mins COOK 20 mins   SERVES 4

- 1 tbsp rapeseed oil
- 1 onion, finely sliced
- 4 skinless boneless chicken thighs, cut into thick strips
- 1–2 tbsp jerk seasoning
- 1 green chilli, deseeded and sliced (optional)
- 2 large garlic cloves, crushed
- 2 x 250g pouches microwave basmati rice, cooked
- 400g can kidney beans, drained and rinsed
- zest and juice 1 lime, plus wedges to serve
- 3 spring onions, finely sliced
- ½ small bunch coriander, finely chopped

1 Heat the oil in a large flameproof casserole dish over a medium-high heat. Add the onion and a pinch of salt and fry for 5–6 mins. Add the chicken and fry for 7–8 mins more. Stir in the jerk seasoning, chilli, if using, and garlic, and cook for 1 min.

2 Stir in the rice, beans and lime zest and juice. Cook until heated through. Scatter over the spring onions and coriander and serve with the extra lime wedges.

Nutrition per serving
energy 411 kcals, fat 11g, saturates 2g, carbs 53g, sugars 4g, fibre 8g, protein 22g, salt 0.8g

Chicken parmigiana

This classic chicken Parmesan recipe gets the *Good Food* makeover, resulting in a hearty yet healthy dish great for sharing with your mates.

 PREP 15 mins COOK 15 mins   SERVES 4

- 2 large skinless chicken breasts, halved through the middle
- 2 eggs, beaten
- 75g breadcrumbs
- 75g Parmesan, grated
- 1 tbsp olive oil
- 2 garlic cloves, crushed
- ½ x 690ml jar passata
- 1 tsp caster sugar
- 1 tsp dried oregano
- ½ x 125g ball light mozzarella

1 Halve the chicken breasts through the middle, then place the 4 pieces between cling film sheets and bash out with a rolling pin until they are the thickness of a £1 coin.

2 Dip in the eggs, then the breadcrumbs mixed with half the grated Parmesan. Set aside on a plate in the fridge while you make the sauce.

3 Heat the olive oil and cook the crushed garlic cloves for 1 min, then tip in half the jar of passata, the caster sugar and oregano. Season and simmer for 5–10 mins.

4 Heat the grill to high and cook the chicken for 5 mins each side, then remove.

5 Pour the tomato sauce into a shallow ovenproof dish and top with the chicken.

6 Scatter over torn pieces of the mozzarella and the remaining grated Parmesan and grill for 3–4 mins until the cheese has melted and the sauce is bubbling.

7 Serve with veg and some potatoes, if you like.

Nutrition per serving
energy 327 kcals, fat 13g, saturates 5g, carbs 22g, sugars 5g, fibre 1g, protein 33g, salt 1.31g

Spiced black bean & chicken soup

Use up leftover roast or ready-cooked chicken in this healthy and warming soup, spiced up with cumin and chilli.

 PREP 10 mins COOK 15 mins   SERVES 4

- 2 tbsp mild olive oil
- 2 fat garlic cloves, crushed
- small bunch coriander stalks, finely chopped, leaves picked
- zest 1 lime, then cut into wedges
- 2 tsp ground cumin
- 1 tsp chilli flakes
- 400g can chopped tomatoes
- 400g can black beans, rinsed and drained
- 600ml chicken stock
- 175g kale, thick stalks removed, leaves shredded
- 50g leftover roast or ready-cooked chicken
- 50g feta, crumbled, to serve
- flour and corn tortillas, toasted, to serve

1 Heat the oil in a large saucepan, add the garlic, coriander stalks and lime zest, then fry for 2 mins until fragrant. Stir in the cumin and chilli flakes, fry for 1 min more, then tip in the tomatoes, beans and stock. Bring to the boil, then crush the beans against the bottom of the pan a few times using a potato masher. This will thicken the soup a little.

2 Stir the kale into the soup, simmer for 5 mins or until tender, then tear in the chicken and let it heat through. Season to taste with salt, pepper and juice from half the lime, then serve in shallow bowls, scattered with the feta and a few coriander leaves. Serve the remaining lime in wedges for the table, with the toasted tortillas on the side. The longer you leave the chicken soup in the pan, the thicker it will become, so add a splash more stock if you can't serve it straight away.

Nutrition per serving
energy 293 kcals, fat 11g, saturates 2g, carbs 15g, sugars 3g, fibre 6g, protein 26g, salt 1g

Spicy chicken couscous

This quick one-pot dish is perfect for a summer supper.

 PREP 15 mins COOK 15 mins   SERVES 4

- 250g couscous
- 3 tbsp olive oil
- 1 onion, chopped
- 2 large skinless chicken breasts, sliced
- 85g blanched almonds
- 1 tbsp hot curry paste
- 100g halved ready-to-eat apricots
- 120g pack coriander

1 Prepare the couscous with chicken stock, according to the packet instructions. Heat the olive oil in a pan and cook the onion for 2–3 mins until softened.
2 Toss in the chicken breast slices and stir-fry for 5–6 mins until tender. Add the blanched almonds and, when golden, stir in the hot curry paste and cook for 1 min more.
3 Add the couscous along with the apricots and the coriander. Toss until hot then serve with plain yogurt, if you like.

Nutrition per serving
energy 486 kcals, fat 23g, saturates 2g, carbs 45g, sugars 0g, fibre 4g, protein 28g, salt 0.56g

Crispy chicken & asparagus pie

Make a super healthy, super tasty crispy chicken and asparagus pie in 20 minutes.

 PREP 10 mins COOK 20 mins   SERVES 4

- 4 skinless chicken breasts, cut into bite-sized pieces
- knob butter
- 100g asparagus, cut into bite-sized pieces
- 100g spring green vegetables (we used baby spinach and defrosted peas)
- 100g ham, torn
- 100ml low-fat crème fraîche
- 50g fresh breadcrumbs

1 Heat the grill to medium. Spread the chicken out evenly in a shallow baking dish. Dot with half the butter and grill for 7–10 mins, turning occasionally until cooked through

2 Meanwhile, put the vegetables in a bowl and pour a kettle of boiling water over them. Leave for 2–3 mins, then drain.

3 Scatter the veg and ham over the chicken, dollop on the crème fraîche and season to taste. Sprinkle on the breadcrumbs, dot with the remaining butter, then slide under the grill for 5 mins more until heated through and the topping is crisp.

Nutrition per serving
energy 300 kcals, fat 9g, saturates 5g, carbs 13g, sugars 0g, fibre 1g, protein 43g, salt 1.21g

Harissa-spiced chicken & bulgur wheat

This spicy harissa dish, with chicken and apricots, takes under 30 mins to bring together.

 PREP 10 mins COOK 20 mins  SERVES 4

- 1 tbsp harissa paste
- 4 skinless chicken breasts
- 1 tbsp vegetable or sunflower oil
- 1 onion, halved and sliced
- 2 tbsp pine nuts
- handful ready-to-eat apricots
- 300g bulgur wheat
- 600ml hot chicken stock (from a cube)
- handful coriander, leaves only, chopped

1 Rub the harissa paste over the chicken. Heat the oil in a deep non-stick pan, then fry the chicken for about 3 mins on each side, until just golden (it won't be cooked through at this stage). Remove and set aside.

2 Add the onion, then gently fry for 5 mins until soft. Tip in the pine nuts and continue cooking for another few mins until toasted. Tip in the apricots, bulgur and stock, then season and cover. Cook for about 10 mins until the stock is almost absorbed.

3 Return the chicken to the pan, re-cover and cook for 5 mins on a low heat until the liquid has been absorbed and the chicken is cooked through. Fluff up the bulgur with a fork and scatter with the coriander to serve.

Nutrition per serving
energy 536 kcals, fat 11g, saturates 2g, carbs 65g, sugars 8g, fibre 2g, protein 49g, salt 1.06g

Lemon & yogurt chicken flatbreads

Make these family-friendly chicken wraps with a lemon, garlic and cinnamon marinade on a barbecue if the sun is shining. Serve in flatbreads with yogurt.

 PREP 20 mins COOK 10 mins   SERVES 4

- 2 skinless chicken breasts, cut into strips
- 1 lemon
- 1 tsp dried oregano (optional)
- 1 garlic clove, crushed
- pinch cinnamon
- 1 tbsp olive oil
- 4 flatbreads
- 4 tbsp Greek yogurt
- ¼ red pepper, finely chopped
- 1 Little Gem lettuce, finely chopped

1 Put the chicken in a bowl. Pare strips of zest from the lemon using a vegetable peeler, then juice the lemon too. Add the peel and half the juice to the chicken, along with the oregano (if using), garlic, cinnamon and oil. Mix well, cover and chill for an hour. The lemon juice will start to 'cook' the chicken, so don't leave for longer.

2 Heat the barbecue until the coals are white. If you are indoors, heat a griddle pan. Thread the chicken strips onto a couple of metal skewers to stop them falling through the grate (you don't need to do this for the griddle), then grill for a couple of mins each side – they'll cook through quickly. Season if you like.

3 Warm the flatbreads on the edge of the barbecue (or on the griddle) for a minute, then transfer them to plates and spread each with ½ tbsp yogurt. Divide the chicken strips between them, then dot on the remaining yogurt and sprinkle over the pepper and lettuce. Fold or roll the flatbreads to eat.

Nutrition per serving
energy 364 kcals, fat 9g, saturates 4g, carbs 41g, sugars 5g, fibre 4g, protein 28g, salt 0.6g

Turkey tortilla pie

Top a chilli con carne with snipped tortilla wraps for this healthy one-pot that fuses nachos with enchiladas.

 PREP 5 mins COOK 25 mins   SERVES 4

- 2 onions, finely chopped
- 1 tbsp olive oil, plus a little extra if needed
- 2 tsp ground cumin
- 500g turkey mince
- 1½ tbsp chipotle paste
- 400g can chopped tomatoes
- 400g can kidney beans, drained and rinsed
- 198g can sweetcorn, drained
- 2 corn tortillas, snipped into triangles
- small handful grated cheddar
- 2 spring onions, finely sliced

1 In a deep flameproof casserole dish, cook the onion in the oil for 8 mins until soft. Add the cumin and cook for 1 min more. Stir in the turkey mince and add a bit more oil, if needed. Turn up the heat and cook for 4–6 mins, stirring occasionally, until the mince is browned.

2 Stir in the chipotle paste, tomatoes and half a can of water, and simmer for 5 mins. Mix in the beans and sweetcorn, and cook for a few mins more until thick, piping hot and the mince is cooked.

3 Heat the grill. Take the pan off the heat and put the tortilla triangles randomly on top. Scatter over the cheese and grill for a few mins until the topping is crisp, taking care that it doesn't burn. Sprinkle with the spring onions and serve.

Nutrition per serving
energy 420 kcals, fat 12g, saturates 4g, carbs 33g, sugars 11g, fibre 8g, protein 42g, salt 1g

Turkey meatballs with couscous

Lighter than pasta and packed with protein, these meatballs make for a satisfying and super healthy supper.

 PREP 15 mins COOK 15 mins   SERVES 4

- 500g turkey mince
- 2 tsp each chilli powder, ground cumin and ground coriander
- 1 tsp ground cinnamon
- 1 onion, coarsely grated
- zest 1 orange, then peeled and orange segments chopped
- 250g couscous
- 250ml hot chicken stock
- 2 tsp olive oil
- small bunch coriander, roughly chopped

1 In a big bowl, mix the mince, spices, onion and orange zest together really well with your hands. Roll the mixture into about 20 walnut-sized meatballs.

2 Put the couscous in a bowl, pour over the hot chicken stock, cover with cling film and leave to stand for 10 mins.

3 Heat the olive oil in a frying pan. Add the meatballs and fry them, turning often, for about 12 mins until browned all over and cooked through.

4 Fluff the couscous up with a fork, stir in the chopped orange, coriander and some seasoning. Pile onto plates and serve with the meatballs.

Nutrition per serving
energy 348 kcals, fat 6g, saturates 1g, carbs 41g, sugars 6g, fibre 1g, protein 36g, salt 0.45g

Turkey curry

Go classic with your turkey leftovers and whip up this healthy spice-filled stew with peppers and tomatoes.

 PREP 5 mins COOK 15 mins  SERVES 4

- 1 tbsp sunflower oil
- 1 large onion, thickly sliced
- 1 green pepper, deseeded and chopped
- 2 tbsp curry paste (or gluten-free alternative)
- 2 garlic cloves, crushed
- 400g can chopped tomatoes
- 300g leftover turkey, diced
- 300g leftover cooked potato (either boiled or roast), diced
- 2 tbsp mango chutney
- small pack coriander, roughly chopped
- rice or naan bread, to serve

1 Heat the oil in a large pan over a fairly high heat. Cook the onion and green pepper for 3–4 mins until starting to soften and brown slightly. Stir in the curry paste and garlic, then cook for another 1–2 mins. Add the chopped tomatoes and 150ml water. Bring to the boil and bubble for 5 mins.

2 Turn the heat down, stir in the turkey and potatoes, and cook for another 2–3 mins, then season and add the mango chutney. Scatter with coriander and serve with rice or naan.

Nutrition per serving
energy 294 kcals, fat 10g, saturates 2g, carbs 26g, sugars 11g, fibre 4g, protein 26g, salt 0.8g

Thai turkey stir-fry

A flash-in-the-pan noodle dish that's flavoursome, low fat and fast for those with a busy schedule.

 PREP 10 mins COOK 15 mins SERVES 4

- 300g rice noodles
- 1 tsp sunflower oil
- 400g turkey breast steaks, cut into thin strips and any fat removed
- 340g green beans, trimmed and halved
- 1 red onion, sliced
- 2 garlic cloves, sliced
- juice 1 lime, plus extra wedges to serve
- 1 tsp chilli powder
- 1 red chilli, finely chopped
- 1 tbsp fish sauce
- handful mint, roughly chopped
- handful coriander, roughly chopped

1 Cook the rice noodles following the packet instructions. Heat the oil in a non-stick pan and fry the turkey over a high heat for 2 mins. Add the beans, onion and garlic, and cook for a further 5 mins.

2 Stir in the lime juice, chilli powder, fresh chilli and fish sauce, then cook for 3 mins more. Stir in the noodles and herbs, then toss everything together before serving.

Nutrition per serving
energy 425 kcals, fat 3g, saturates 1g, carbs 71g, sugars 4g, fibre 4g, protein 32g, salt 0.92g

Turkey & coriander burgers

These healthy burgers are full of vitamin C and use low-fat turkey flavoured with herbs and topped with spicy avocado.

 PREP 15 mins COOK 15 mins   SERVES 4

- 400g turkey mince
- 1 tsp Worcestershire sauce
- 85g fresh breadcrumbs
- 1 tbsp chopped coriander
- 1 red onion, finely chopped
- 1 large ripe avocado or 2 small
- 1 chilli, deseeded and finely chopped
- juice 1 lime
- 4 ciabatta rolls, cut in half
- 1 tsp sunflower oil
- 8 hot peppers from a jar, roughly chopped

1 Mix the mince, Worcestershire sauce, breadcrumbs, half each of the coriander and onion, and some seasoning until combined. Form into 4 burgers, then chill until ready to cook.

2 To make the guacamole, mash the avocado with the remaining coriander and onion, the chilli and lime juice, and season.

3 Heat a griddle pan or barbecue until hot. Griddle the ciabatta rolls, cut side down, for 1 min, then keep warm. Brush the burgers with the oil to keep them from sticking. Cook for 7–8 mins on each side until charred and cooked through. Fill the rolls with the burgers, guacamole and peppers.

Nutrition per serving
energy 497 kcals, fat 15g, saturates 3g, carbs 51g, sugars 7g, fibre 6g, protein 40g, salt 1.3g

Cajun turkey salad with guacamole

This quick supper is great for a warm evening eating outside. Make your own guacamole if you have time.

 PREP 15 mins COOK 10 mins SERVES 4

- 2 tbsp sesame seeds
- 2 tbsp groundnut or sunflower oil
- 500g turkey breast steaks, cut into strips
- 1 tbsp Cajun seasoning
- 1 large red pepper, deseeded, quartered and sliced
- 120g bag herb salad
- 130g tub guacamole
- 200g bag tortilla chips

1 Heat a large frying pan or wok, sprinkle in the sesame seeds and toss them over a fairly high heat for about a minute until they're slightly golden. Add the oil to the pan or wok, tip in the turkey, Cajun seasoning and red pepper and stir-fry for about 5 minutes until the turkey turns from pink to white.

2 While the turkey's sizzling, divide the herb salad between 4 dinner plates then, as soon as the turkey's done, spoon it over the salad, making sure to include all the spicy juices. Top each serving with a spoonful of guacamole, pile tortilla chips on the side of each plate and serve.

Nutrition per serving
energy 524 kcals, fat 27g, saturates 5g, carbs 35g, sugars 0g, fibre 5g, protein 37g, salt 1.37g

Turkey burgers with beetroot relish

Treat yourself to these low-fat, healthy burgers after a hard day's work. They are quick and easy to make.

 PREP 15 mins COOK 15 mins   SERVES 4

- 500g turkey mince
- ½ tsp dried thyme or 2 tsp fresh
- 1 lemon

FOR THE RELISH

- 250g cooked peeled beetroot (not in vinegar), finely diced
- 1 small red onion, finely chopped
- 2 tbsp chopped parsley
- 2 tsp olive oil
- 2 tsp wholegrain mustard
- Little Gem lettuce, to serve
- wholemeal pitta breads, to serve

1 Tip the turkey into a bowl with the thyme. Finely grate in the zest from the lemon and add a little seasoning. Use your hands to mix the ingredients well, then shape into 4 patties. Chill until ready to cook. Can be frozen for up to 1 month.

2 Mix the beetroot with the juice from half the lemon, the onion, parsley, oil and mustard. Grill, griddle or barbecue the burgers for about 6 mins each side and serve with the beetroot relish, lettuce and pitta breads.

Nutrition per serving
energy 183 kcals, fat 4g, saturates 1g, carbs 7g, sugars 6g, fibre 2g, protein 30g, salt 0.5g

Chapter 2

MEAT

· ·

In this chapter, you'll find a range of ways to cook your favourite meats. From teriyaki steak and pork meatballs to grilled lamb, these recipes will help you discover delicious ways to enjoy healthy meat dishes, and they can all be made in under 30 minutes. Red meats are a great way to add more iron to your diet, as well as vitamin B12 and zinc.

Broccoli pesto & pancetta pasta

Serve this healthy bowl of pasta topped with cherry tomatoes for a quick and easy midweek meal. It's tossed with broccoli pesto, and takes just 25 minutes to make.

 PREP 10 mins COOK 15 mins   SERVES 4

- 300g broccoli, broken into florets
- 300g pasta (we used orecchiette)
- 1 tbsp pine nuts
- large bunch basil
- 1 large garlic clove
- 2 tbsp finely grated Parmesan
- 1 tbsp olive oil
- 50g smoked pancetta, diced
- 200g cherry tomatoes, halved

1 Bring a pan of lightly salted water to the boil. Add the broccoli and boil for 5 mins. Scoop out with a slotted spoon and set aside.

2 Put the pasta in the same pan and cook following packet instructions. Meanwhile, tip the broccoli into a food processor with the pine nuts, basil, garlic, Parmesan and oil, and blitz until smooth. Season with black pepper and a little salt (the pancetta is very salty).

3 Set a frying pan over a medium heat and cook the pancetta for 2 mins. Add the tomatoes and cook for 3 mins, or until softened. Toss the pasta with the broccoli pesto, tomatoes and pancetta, and loosen with a splash of pasta water, if needed. Spoon into bowls and serve.

Nutrition per serving
energy 452 kcals, fat 14g, saturates 4g, carbs 60g, sugars 5g, fibre 7g, protein 19g, salt 0.5g

Pork souvlaki

Serve our speedy pork souvlaki skewers when you're in need of a quick and easy midweek meal. Serve with flatbreads and yogurt and chilli sauce on the side.

 PREP 15 mins COOK 10 mins   SERVES 4

- 400g lean pork shoulder, cut into 2cm chunks
- 1 tbsp olive oil
- ½ tbsp dried oregano
- zest and juice of 1 lemon
- ½ tsp hot paprika
- 100ml fat-free yogurt
- 1 small garlic clove, grated
- ½ cucumber, trimmed and grated
- 2 red peppers, deseeded and cut into chunks
- 2 Little Gem lettuce, leaves separated
- chilli sauce, to serve (optional)
- flatbreads, warmed, to serve (optional)

1 Put the pork in a large bowl with the oil, oregano, lemon zest and juice and paprika as well as a good pinch of salt. Toss everything together to combine and leave to marinate for 10 mins.

2 Combine the yogurt, garlic and cucumber together in a bowl. Season with salt and set aside.

3 Heat the grill to high. Thread the marinated pork and the peppers on 4 metal skewers, alternating between the pork and peppers as you go. Place on a non-stick baking sheet and grill for 3–4 mins on each side, or until cooked through and golden brown.

4 Serve with the lettuce, yogurt mixture and chilli sauce, and flatbreads, if you like.

Nutrition per serving
energy 210 kcals, fat 8g, saturates 2g, carbs 8g, sugars 8g, fibre 5g, protein 25g, salt 0.3g

Pan-fried pork with maple & mustard

Pork tenderloins are good value and are always very tender and moist, as long as you take care not to overcook them. Serve this dish with saffron rice.

 PREP 10 mins COOK 20 mins SERVES 4

- 2 pork tenderloins, about 300g each
- 1 tbsp plain flour
- 2 tbsp olive oil
- 1 red onion, thinly sliced
- 200ml vegetable stock
- 2 tbsp maple syrup
- 2 tbsp wholegrain mustard
- juice 1 lemon
- handful parsley sprigs (optional)

1 Cut the pork into 3cm thick slices, season with salt and pepper, then lightly coat in the flour (the easiest way to do this is to put the flour and seasoning in a large food bag, add the pork and shake well). Heat the oil in a large frying pan, preferably non-stick, then add the pork and quickly fry until it is browned all over. Cook the pork for about 5 mins, then remove to a plate and cover with foil while you make the sauce.

2 Add the onion to the pan (with a touch more oil if needed), then quickly fry until lightly coloured. Add the stock, then bring to the boil. Boil hard for a couple of minutes to reduce the stock a little, stir in the maple syrup, mustard and lemon juice, then bring back to the boil, stirring well.

3 Return the pork to the pan and gently simmer for a further 3–4 mins until it is cooked through. Sprinkle with parsley, if using.

Nutrition per serving
energy 327 kcals, fat 16g, saturates 4g, carbs 11g, sugars 7g, fibre 1g, protein 35g, salt 0.58g

Prosciutto, kale & butter bean stew

Whip up this healthy stew in just 25 minutes with prosciutto, kale and butter beans. It's a low-calorie, low-fat dinner with 3 of your 5-a-day.

 PREP 5 mins COOK 20 mins   SERVES 4

- 80g pack prosciutto, torn into pieces
- 2 tbsp olive oil
- 1 fennel bulb, sliced
- 2 garlic cloves, crushed
- 1 tsp chilli flakes
- 4 thyme sprigs
- 150ml white wine or chicken stock
- 2 x 400g cans butter beans
- 400g can cherry tomatoes
- 200g bag sliced kale

1 Fry the prosciutto in a dry saucepan over a high heat until crisp, then remove half with a slotted spoon and set aside. Turn the heat down to low, pour in the oil and tip in the fennel with a pinch of salt. Cook for 5 mins until softened, then throw in the garlic, chilli flakes and thyme and cook for a further 2 mins, then pour in the wine or stock and bring to a simmer.

2 Tip both cans of butter beans into the stew, along with their liquid, then add the tomatoes, season well and bring everything to a simmer. Cook, undisturbed, for 5 mins, then stir through the kale. Once wilted, ladle the stew into bowls, removing the thyme sprigs and topping each portion with the remaining prosciutto.

Nutrition per serving
energy 290 kcals, fat 9g, saturates 2g, carbs 23g, sugars 6g, fibre 12g, protein 16g, salt 1.2g

Sweet & spicy pan-fry pork & noodles

Whip up some healthy fast-food with a pork pan fry - on the table in 10 minutes.

 PREP 2 mins COOK 8 mins   SERVES 4

- 6 spring onions
- 2 tbsp sunflower oil
- 300g bag small broccoli florets
- ½ pack thick egg noodle
- 450g pack lean pork stir-fry strips
- 100g shiitake or chestnut mushrooms
- 180g jar Cantonese sweet and spicy stir-fry sauce
- 300g bag beansprouts
- handful roasted salted cashew nuts

1 Over a high heat, bring a pan of water to the boil (for the noodles). Chop the onions into chunky lengths. Heat the oil in a wok, tip in the broccoli and stir-fry for 2 minutes until it starts to soften.

2 Tip the noodles into the boiling water and boil for 4 minutes until softened. Meanwhile, add the pork strips to the wok and fry until the meat changes colour. Add the onions and mushrooms and cook for a minute or so until the mushrooms start to soften.

3 Stir in the sauce until everything is well coated. Drain the noodles and toss into the wok with the beansprouts and cashews. Heat until the beansprouts start to soften slightly then serve.

Nutrition per serving
energy 423 kcals, fat 18g, saturates 2g, carbs 32g, sugars 0g, fibre 4g, protein 37g, salt 0.87g

Thai green pork lettuce cups

A healthy, quick and simple midweek meal with fragrant Thai flavours, pork and lots of fresh herbs.

 PREP 10 mins COOK 15 mins  SERVES 4

- 1 tbsp sesame oil
- 500g pork mince
- 1 tbsp Thai green curry paste
- 1 red onion, finely chopped
- juice 1 lime
- 1 tbsp fish sauce
- ½ small pack mint, leaves only, roughly chopped
- ½ small pack coriander, leaves only, roughly chopped
- 4 Little Gem lettuces, leaves separated
- rice, to serve (optional)

1 Heat the oil in a frying pan and cook the pork for 8–10 mins or until cooked through. Stir in the green curry paste and 2 tbsp water, then cook for 1–2 mins.

2 Remove from the heat and stir in the red onion, lime juice, fish sauce and herbs. Spoon the pork into the lettuce leaves and serve with rice, if you like.

Nutrition per serving
energy 298 kcals, fat 17g, saturates 5g, carbs 7g, sugars 6g, fibre 3g, protein 27g, salt 1.1g

Pork with sweet & sour onion sauce

This healthy, meaty main uses lean pork fillet and is on the table in just 30 minutes – serve with your choice of grain.

 PREP 10 mins COOK 20 mins SERVES 4

- 250g mixed basmati rice and wild rice
- 600g pork fillet, cut into 4cm slices
- 2 tbsp coarse black pepper (freshly ground)
- 2 tbsp olive oil
- 1 large red onion, halved and sliced
- 150ml cider vinegar
- 75ml maple syrup
- small bunch parsley, chopped

1 Boil the rice in plenty of water, following the packet instructions, until cooked. Drain, return to the pot and cover to keep warm.

2 Meanwhile, sprinkle the meat on all sides with the black pepper and some salt. Heat 1 tbsp of the oil in a large frying pan. Sear the meat on both sides until nicely browned. Remove from the pan.

3 Add the remaining oil and the onion to the pan. Cook for 5 mins, then pour in the vinegar and let reduce for 1 min. Stir in the maple syrup, then return the pork to the pan and heat for 5 mins until cooked through. Serve the pork and sauce spooned over the rice and scattered with the parsley.

Nutrition per serving
energy 574 kcals, fat 16g, saturates 4g, carbs 61g, sugars 15g, fibre 3g, protein 41g, salt 0.2g

Lemon & rosemary pork with chickpeas

Jazz up pork with lemon and rosemary for a feel-good supper that's on the table in under half an hour.

 PREP 10 mins COOK 15 mins SERVES 4

- 1 tbsp olive oil
- 2 tsp finely chopped rosemary
- 4 cloves garlic, crushed
- juice and zest ½ lemon
- 4 boneless pork steaks, fat trimmed
- 1 red onion, finely sliced
- 2 tbsp sherry vinegar
- 2 x 400g cans chickpeas, rinsed and drained
- 110g bag mixed salad leaves

1 Mix the olive oil, rosemary, garlic, lemon juice and zest in a large bowl. Add the pork, turn to coat and season well. If you have time, marinate in the fridge for 30 mins.

2 Heat a large non-stick frying pan. Lift the pork out of the marinade, shaking off any excess and reserving the marinade for later. Cook the pork in the pan for 3–4 mins each side or until cooked through. Rest on a plate while you make the salad.

3 Pour the reserved marinade into the pan with the onion. Cook for 1 min over a high heat before adding the vinegar, plus 3 tbsp water. Bubble down for 1 min, until the onion has softened a little and the dressing thickened slightly. Stir through chickpeas, some salt and pepper and any of the resting juices from the pork. Put salad leaves into a bowl, tip in the pan contents and gently toss, before eating immediately with the pork.

Nutrition per serving
energy 396 kcals, fat 17g, saturates 3g, carbs 23g, sugars 3g, fibre 6g, protein 40g, salt 0.9g

Jerk-seasoned pork pineapple skewers

Pop these healthy kebabs on a griddle or the BBQ – they're packed with Creole spices and are a lean treat.

 PREP 10 mins COOK 15 mins   SERVES 4

- 400g pork fillet, cut into 4cm chunks
- 2 tbsp jerk or Creole seasoning
- 1 tsp ground allspice
- 1 tbsp hot chilli sauce, plus extra to serve (optional)
- 3 limes, zest and juice 1, other 2 cut into wedges to serve
- ½ small pineapple, peeled, cored and cut into 4cm chunks
- 1 tbsp vegetable oil
- 200g basmati rice
- 400g can black beans, drained and rinsed

1 Mix the pork, jerk seasoning, allspice, chilli sauce, if using, lime zest and juice, and some seasoning together. Thread the pork and pineapple onto metal skewers (or pre-soaked wooden skewers) and brush with the oil.

2 Cook the rice following packet instructions. Drain well, then put back in the saucepan with the beans, stir and keep warm.

3 Meanwhile, heat a griddle pan until very hot. Cook the skewers for 3 mins on each side until nicely charred and the pork is cooked through. Serve the skewers with the beans and rice, extra chilli sauce, if you like, and lime wedges for squeezing over.

Nutrition per serving
energy 451 kcals, fat 10g, saturates 3g, carbs 57g, sugars 7g, fibre 6g, protein 30g, salt 0.2g

Crisp sage & Parmesan pork with slaw

Perk up some pork with this full-flavoured sage and red apple coleslaw recipe

 PREP 15 mins COOK 10 mins   SERVES 4

- 4 x 175g pork loin steaks, fat trimmed
- 2 slices white bread
- handful sage leaves
- 25g Parmesan, finely grated
- 1 egg, beaten
- 1 tbsp oil
- ½ white cabbage, core removed, finely shredded
- 4 tbsp buttermilk or low-fat natural yogurt
- 2 red-skinned apples, halved and sliced
- lemon wedges, to serve (optional)

1 Lay the pork steaks between 2 sheets of cling film or baking paper and bash with a rolling pin until approx 1cm thick. Whizz the bread in a food processor to make breadcrumbs. Add the sage and pulse a few more times to roughly chop the leaves. Mix in the Parmesan and spread over a large plate. Season with black pepper.

2 One by one, dip each pork steak into the beaten egg, allow the excess to drip off, then press into the breadcrumb mix on both sides. Set aside.

3 Heat the oil in a large non-stick frying pan and fry the steaks for 3–4 mins on each side until cooked through. Meanwhile, mix the cabbage, buttermilk or yogurt and apple, then season. Serve the steaks with the coleslaw and a lemon wedge, if using, for squeezing over.

Nutrition per serving
energy 380 kcals, fat 13g, saturates 4g, carbs 21g, sugars 12g, fibre 3g, protein 47g, salt 0.7g

Meatball & tomato soup

Get 3 of your 5-a-day in one serving with this healthy, low-calorie tomato soup. The addition of meatballs and giant couscous means it's filling, too.

 PREP 5 mins COOK 15 mins   SERVES 4

- 1½ tbsp rapeseed oil
- 1 onion, finely chopped
- 2 red peppers, deseeded and sliced
- 1 garlic clove, crushed
- ½ tsp chilli flakes
- 2 x 400g cans chopped tomatoes
- 100g giant couscous
- 500ml hot vegetable stock
- 12 pork meatballs
- 150g baby spinach
- ½ small bunch basil
- grated Parmesan, to serve (optional)

1 Heat the oil in a saucepan. Fry the onion and peppers for 7 mins, then stir through the garlic and chilli flakes and cook for 1 min. Add the tomatoes, giant couscous and veg stock and bring to a simmer.

2 Season to taste, then add the meatballs and spinach. Simmer for 5–7 mins or until cooked through. Ladle into bowls and top with the basil and some Parmesan, if you like.

Nutrition per serving
energy 330 kcals, fat 12g, saturates 3g, carbs 36g, sugars 14g, fibre 6g, protein 17g, salt 0.7g

Teriyaki steak with fennel slaw

This flavoursome steak and salad dish is low in fat and easy to make.

 PREP 15 mins COOK 5 mins   SERVES 4

- 2 tbsp low-salt soy sauce
- 1 tbsp red wine vinegar
- 1 tsp clear honey
- 4 sirloin or rump steaks, trimmed of all visible fat, each about 125g

FOR THE FENNEL SLAW
- 1 large carrot, coarsely grated
- 1 fennel bulb, halved and thinly sliced
- 1 red onion, halved and thinly sliced
- handful coriander leaves
- juice 1 lime

1 Mix the soy, vinegar and honey, add the steaks, then marinate for 10–15 mins.

2 Toss together the carrot, fennel, onion and coriander, then chill until ready to serve.

3 Cook the steaks in a griddle pan for a few mins on each side, depending on the thickness and how well done you like them. Set the meat aside to rest on a plate, then add the remaining marinade to the pan. Bubble the marinade until it reduces a little to make a sticky sauce.

4 Dress the salad with the lime juice, then pile onto plates and serve with the steaks. Spoon the sauce over the meat.

Nutrition per serving
energy 188 kcals, fat 5g, saturates 2g, carbs 7g, sugars 6g, fibre 2g, protein 29g, salt 1.05g

Italian-style beef stew

An easy, super healthy stew full of vitamin C.

 PREP 10 mins COOK 20 mins   SERVES 4

- 1 onion, sliced
- 1 garlic clove, sliced
- 2 tbsp olive oil
- 300g pack beef stir-fry strips, or use beef steak, thinly sliced
- 1 yellow pepper, deseeded and thinly sliced
- 400g can chopped tomatoes
- sprig rosemary, chopped
- handful pitted olives

1 In a large saucepan, cook the onion and garlic in olive oil for 5 mins until softened and turning golden. Tip in the beef strips, pepper, tomatoes and rosemary, then bring to the boil. Simmer for 15 mins until the meat is cooked through, adding some boiling water if needed. Stir through the olives and serve with mash or polenta.

Nutrition per serving
energy 225 kcals, fat 11g, saturates 3g, carbs 7g, sugars 6g, fibre 2g, protein 25g, salt 0.87g

Quick beef & broccoli one-pot

Create a delicious beef and broccoli meal in one pot, fast! Contains 2 of your 5-a-day.

 PREP 10 mins COOK 10 mins  SERVES 4

- 1 tbsp olive oil
- 50g unsalted cashew nuts
- 400g frying beef steak, cut into strips
- 1 large broccoli, broken into florets
- 4 sticks celery, sliced
- 150ml beef stock (from a cube is fine)
- 2 tbsp horseradish sauce
- 2 tbsp low-fat fromage frais

1 Heat the oil in a frying pan, add the nuts and toss for a few secs until lightly toasted. Set aside.

2 Season the steak strips with plenty of pepper and stir-fry over a high heat for 1–2 mins to brown. Set aside with the nuts. Tip the broccoli and celery into the pan and stir-fry for 2 mins. Pour the stock over, cover and simmer for 2 mins. Meanwhile, mix the horseradish and fromage frais together.

3 Return the steak to the pan and toss with the veg, then sprinkle over the nuts and serve with the creamy horseradish. Great with mashed potatoes.

Nutrition per serving
energy 269 kcals, fat 14g, saturates 3g, carbs 6g, sugars 4g, fibre 3g, protein 29g, salt 0.54g

Lamb meatballs & tahini tabbouleh

Combine grains and beetroot with lamb meatballs and a tahini dressing to make this quick and easy supper, which is full of textures and flavours.

 PREP 15 mins COOK 15 mins   SERVES 4

- 2 tbsp tahini
- 2 tbsp fat-free yogurt
- ½ small bunch parsley
- juice 1 lemon
- ½ small garlic clove
- ½ tbsp rapeseed oil
- 10–12 ready-made lamb meatballs
- 2 x 250g pouches mixed grains
- 4 cooked beetroots, chopped
- 2 spring onions, sliced
- 200g baby tomatoes, halved
- 50g pitted black olives, halved
- 1 cucumber, peeled and cubed
- ½ tbsp za'atar

1 Blend the tahini, yogurt, parsley, lemon juice, garlic, 2–3 tbsp water and a pinch of salt in a food processor until smooth. Set aside.
2 Heat the oil in a non-stick frying pan and cook the meatballs over a medium heat for about 10–12 mins until cooked through, turning regularly.
3 Warm the grains following the packet instructions. Leave to cool a little, then toss with the remaining ingredients. Season. Divide between 4 plates, top with the meatballs and drizzle over the tahini dressing.

Nutrition per serving
energy 502 kcals, fat 23g, saturates 5g, carbs 46g, sugars 9g, fibre 9g, protein 24g, salt 0.92g

Lamb & squash biryani with raita

Cook our healthy lamb curry with butternut squash for a tasty, filling dinner. It's low-calorie, rich in iron and provides three of your 5-a-day.

 PREP 10 mins COOK 20 mins   SERVES 4

- 4 lean lamb steaks (about 400g), trimmed of all fat, cut into chunks
- 2 garlic cloves, finely grated
- 8 tsp chopped fresh ginger
- 3 tsp ground coriander
- 4 tsp rapeseed oil
- 4 onions, sliced
- 2 red chillies, deseeded and chopped
- 170g brown basmati rice
- 320g diced butternut squash
- 2 tsp cumin seeds
- 2 tsp vegetable bouillon powder
- 20cm length cucumber, grated
- 100ml bio yogurt
- 4 tbsp chopped mint, plus a few extra leaves
- handful coriander, chopped

1 Mix the lamb with the garlic, 2 tsp chopped ginger and 1 tsp ground coriander and set aside.

2 Heat 2 tsp oil in a non-stick pan. Add the onions, the remaining ginger and chilli and stir-fry briefly over a high heat so they start to soften. Add the rice and squash and stir over the heat for a few mins. Tip in all the remaining spices, then stir in 500ml boiling water and the bouillon. Cover the pan and simmer for 20 mins.

3 Meanwhile, mix the cucumber, yogurt and mint together in a bowl to make a raita. Chill half for later.

4 About 5 mins before the rice is ready, heat the remaining oil in a non-stick frying pan, add the lamb and stir for a few mins until browned but still nice and tender. Toss into the spiced rice with the coriander and serve with the raita and a few mint or coriander leaves on top.

Nutrition per serving
energy 463 kcals, fat 15g, saturates 4g, carbs 49g, sugars 12g, fibre 7g, protein 30g, salt 0.4g

Chapter 3

WHITE FISH

· ·

White fish, such as cod, haddock and monkfish, are wonderful sources of lean protein for those looking to monitor their fat intake. With their neutral flavour, they're the perfect base ingredient for the delicious herb and spice combinations you'll find in our recipes. Explore lovely curries, simply stews and zesty roasts.

Turmeric, ginger & coconut fish curry

Serve up this healthy fish curry, with vibrant turmeric, ginger and coconut flavours, for an easy midweek meal. It takes just 30 minutes from prep to plate.

 PREP 5 mins COOK 25 mins   SERVES 4

- 1 tbsp olive oil
- 2 onions, finely sliced
- thumb-sized piece ginger, grated
- ½ tbsp turmeric
- 1 tbsp garam masala
- ½ tsp cayenne
- 325ml light coconut milk
- 400g skinless cod loin, cut into chunks
- 300g frozen peas
- 300g sugar snap peas
- 400g brown basmati rice, cooked, to serve
- 1 red chilli, finely sliced
- 1 lime, cut into wedges, to serve

1 Heat the oil in a large saucepan over a medium heat, then fry the onion for 8 mins until translucent. Stir in the ginger and spices and cook for another minute. Pour in the coconut milk and 100ml water, stir, then simmer for 10 mins.

2 Add the cod, frozen peas and sugar snap peas, and simmer for 5 mins until the fish is flaky. Serve with the rice, sliced chilli, a good grinding of black pepper and some lime wedges on the side for squeezing over.

Nutrition per serving
energy 409 kcals, fat 12g, saturates 6g, carbs 44g, sugars 11g, fibre 7g, protein 28g, salt 0.3g

Jamaican beer grilled fish

Combine beer, paprika and onion powder for this simple, yet vibrant Caribbean inspired marinade – perfect for snapper or sea bream.

 PREP 5 mins COOK 25 mins   SERVES 4

- 2 medium red snappers or whole bream, gutted, scaled and cleaned
- 1 tbsp onion powder
- 2 tsp sweet smoked paprika
- pinch dried thyme
- 100ml Jamaican beer, plus extra to baste
- 2 limes, 1 sliced, 1 cut into wedges

1 Make a few slashes in the flesh on either side of the fish with a sharp knife. Mix the onion powder, paprika, thyme and some seasoning with the beer. Pour over the fish and rub into the slashes and cavity. Place the lime slices inside the fishes' bellies. If you have time, cover with cling film and leave to marinate in the fridge for 1 hr.

2 Heat the grill to medium-high. Place the fish on a tray and grill for 15–20 mins, depending on the size, turning halfway through. Baste the fish with a little beer as it cooks. Serve with lime wedges to squeeze over.

Nutrition per serving
energy 395 kcals, fat 6g, saturates 1g, carbs 7g, sugars 3g, fibre 1g, protein 79g, salt 0.8g

Fish tacos

Serve lemon sole goujons in Mexican-style soft corn tortillas with red onion, cabbage and coriander salad and a chipotle mayo.

 PREP 15 mins COOK 15 mins   SERVES 4

- 220g pack lemon sole goujons
- 1 tsp chipotle paste or harissa paste
- 6 tbsp mayonnaise
- 4 soft corn tortillas
- 175g white cabbage, finely shredded
- good handful chopped coriander
- 1 small red onion, finely chopped or sliced
- juice 1 small lime, plus wedges to serve (optional)

1 Heat the oven to 220C/200C fan/gas 7. Space the goujons apart on a baking sheet and bake for 12–15 mins, following the pack instructions, until crispy. Meanwhile, mix the chipotle or harissa into the mayo, and warm the tortillas – they are best warmed over a gas flame.

2 To make the salad, toss the cabbage, coriander and onion with the lime juice and some salt.

3 Spread the tortillas with a little spicy mayo, then place the salad and fish down the centre. Top with a little more mayo, then fold and eat with your fingers. Serve with lime wedges, if you like.

Nutrition per serving
energy 312 kcals, fat 15g, saturates 2g, carbs 34g, sugars 5g, fibre 3g, protein 13g, salt 1.2g

Steamed fish with ginger & spring onion

Take a 'no washing-up' approach to low-fat cooking – steam fish with pak choi, mirin, garlic and soy in a foil parcel and serve topped with coriander.

 PREP 10 mins COOK 20 mins   SERVES 4

- 100g pak choi
- 4 x 150g firm white fish fillets
- 5cm piece ginger, finely shredded
- 2 garlic cloves, finely sliced
- 2 tbsp low-salt soy sauce
- 1 tsp mirin rice wine
- bunch spring onions, finely shredded
- handful coriander, chopped
- brown rice, to serve
- 1 lime, cut into wedges, to serve

1 Heat the oven to 200C/180C fan/gas 6. Cut a large rectangle of foil, big enough to make a large envelope. Place the pak choi on the foil, followed by the fish, then the ginger and garlic. Pour over the soy sauce and rice wine, then season.

2 Fold over the foil and seal the 3 edges, then put on a baking sheet. Cook for 20 mins, open the parcel and scatter over the spring onions and coriander. Serve with brown rice and squeezed lime juice.

Nutrition per serving
energy 145 kcals, fat 1g, saturates 0g, carbs 4g, sugars 3g, fibre 1g, protein 29g, salt 1.1g

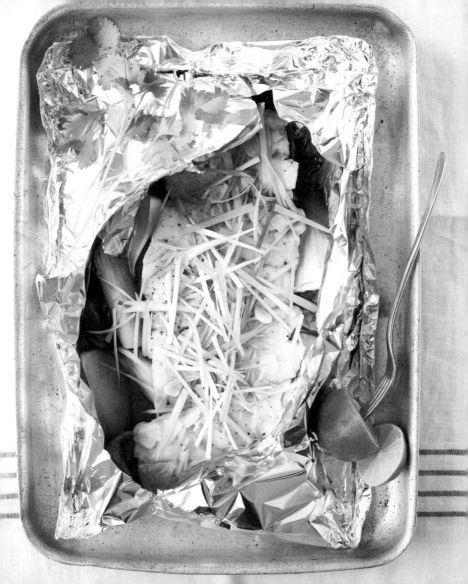

Simple spicy fish stew

Perfect with some crusty bread, this simple healthy stew will soon become a favourite – make it with chicken if you prefer.

 PREP 5 mins COOK 15 mins SERVES 4

- 1 tbsp olive oil
- 2 garlic cloves, crushed
- 1 tsp ground cumin
- ½ tsp paprika
- 200g can chopped tomatoes
- 1 red pepper, deseeded, cut into chunks
- 450g white fish fillets, cut into chunks
- handful coriander, roughly chopped
- 1 lemon, cut into wedges

1 Heat the oil in a saucepan. Tip in the garlic, cumin and paprika and cook for 1 min. Add 100ml water and the tomatoes. Bring to the boil, then turn down the heat. Add the pepper, simmer for 5 mins. Add the fish, simmer for 5 mins. Serve with coriander and a wedge of lemon.

Nutrition per serving
energy 143 kcals, fat 4g, saturates 1g, carbs 5g, sugars 4g, fibre 1g, protein 2g, salt 0.28g

One-pot coconut fish curry

Cook our easy one-pot curry in just half an hour, with only 5 mins prep. It's ideal for feeding the family quickly, on a budget. Serve with rice and yogurt.

 PREP 5 mins COOK 25 mins   SERVES 4

- 1 tbsp rapeseed oil
- 1 onion, chopped
- 1 large garlic clove, crushed
- 1 tsp turmeric
- 1 tsp garam masala
- 1 tsp chilli flakes
- 400ml can coconut milk
- 390g pack fish pie mix
- 200g frozen peas
- 1 lime, cut into wedges
- yogurt and rice, to serve

1 Heat the oil in a large saucepan over a medium heat, add the onion and a big pinch of salt. Gently fry until the onion is translucent, so around 10 mins, then add the garlic and spices. Stir and cook for another minute, adding a splash of water to prevent them sticking. Tip in the coconut milk and stir well, then simmer for 10 mins.

2 Tip the fish pie mix and the frozen peas into the pan and cook until the peas are bright green and the fish is starting the flake, so around 3 mins. Season and add lime juice to taste. Ladle into bowls and serve with yogurt and rice.

Nutrition per serving
energy 352 kcals, fat 23g, saturates 15g, carbs 13g, sugars 7g, fibre 5g, protein 22g, salt 0.6g

Roasted cod with zingy beetroot salad

Make the most of the colour and flavour of beetroot with our easy roasted cod served on a beetroot, new potato and carrot salad with a lovely zingy dressing.

 PREP 10 mins COOK 20 mins   SERVES 4

- 200g baby new potatoes, quartered
- ½ tbsp olive oil
- 4 skinless cod fillets (or any white fish)
- thumb-sized piece ginger, finely sliced
- 1 lime, sliced

FOR THE BEETROOT SALAD

- 1 red onion, finely chopped
- 4 carrots, peeled and grated
- 2 large raw beetroot, peeled and grated
- zest and juice 1 lime
- ½ tbsp honey
- ½ small bunch coriander, leaves picked

1 Heat the oven to 200C/180C fan/gas 6. Put a pan of water on a high heat. When it boils add the potatoes, then turn the heat down and simmer for 10–12 mins until tender.

2 Meanwhile, combine all of the salad ingredients, reserving a little coriander. Season lightly. Once the potatoes are cooked, drain and run under cold water to cool. Drain again and toss through the salad.

3 Rub the oil over the cod fillets, then put on a non-stick baking tray and lay a few ginger and lime slices on top of each fillet. Put in the oven and cook for 6–9 mins, depending on the thickness.

4 Divide the salad between 4 plates, then top with the cod and remaining coriander.

Nutrition per serving
energy 262 kcals, fat 3g, saturates 1g, carbs 21g, sugars 12g, fibre 6g, protein 36g, salt 0.4g

Coriander cod with carrot pilaf

A super healthy supper: low fat and containing a good source of beta-carotene. Great for keeping those healthy resolutions and quick to make too.

 PREP 10 mins COOK 15 mins SERVES 4

- 2 tbsp olive oil
- 4 skinless cod fillets, about 175g each
- 2 tbsp chopped coriander
- zest and juice 1 lemon
- 1 onion, chopped
- 2 tsp cumin seeds
- 2 large carrots, grated
- 200g basmati rice
- 600ml vegetable stock

1 Heat the grill pan to high, then line with double thickness foil and curl up the edges to catch the juices. Brush lightly with oil and put the cod on top. Sprinkle over the coriander, lemon zest and juice and drizzle with a little more of the oil. Season with salt and pepper, then grill for 10–12 mins until the fish flakes easily.

2 Meanwhile, heat the remaining oil in a pan. Add the onion and cumin and fry for a few mins. Add the carrots and stir well, then stir in the rice until glistening. Add the stock and bring to the boil. Cover and cook gently for about 10 mins until the rice is tender and the stock absorbed. Spoon the rice onto 4 warm plates, top with the cod and pour over the pan juices.

Nutrition per serving
energy 305 kcals, fat 7g, saturates 1g. carbs 50g, sugars 8g, fibre 3g, protein 14g, salt 0.31g

Pan-fried fish with zesty polenta crust

If you fancy the crunch of a crust but not the calories, try this healthy recipe, which can be prepared ahead.

 PREP 5 mins COOK 15 mins SERVES 4

- 2 tbsp plain flour
- 4 tbsp fine polenta
- grated zest ½ orange
- 1 tbsp thyme leaves
- 4 skinless white fish fillets
- 1 egg, beaten
- 25g butter
- 2 tbsp olive oil
- 500g baby spinach

1 Mix the flour, polenta, orange zest and thyme leaves together with some seasoning. Dip the fillets in the beaten egg then roll in the polenta mix to coat. The fish can now be chilled for a few hours, if you have time, before cooking.

2 Heat the butter and olive oil in a large frying pan until foaming, add the fillets and lower the heat. Cook for 3 mins on each side. Meanwhile, wilt the spinach in a large pan, drain off the excess water, season and divide between 4 plates. Serve with the fish fillet on top.

Nutrition per serving
energy 331 kcals, fat 14g, saturates 5g, carbs 19g, sugars 0g, fibre 2g, protein 32g, salt 0.57g

Kedgeree with poached egg

This curried fish and rice dish is suitable for brunch, breakfast or as a main course at dinnertime. Replace traditional boiled eggs with poached.

 PREP 5 mins COOK 25 mins  SERVES 4

- 300g long grain rice
- 2 tbsp olive oil
- 1 onion, finely chopped
- 2 garlic cloves, finely chopped
- 390g pack fish pie mix, defrosted if frozen
- 1 heaped tbsp mild or medium curry powder
- juice 1 lemon
- ¼ small pack parsley, chopped
- 4 eggs

1 Cook the rice according to the packet instructions, then drain and set aside. Meanwhile, heat 1 tbsp of the oil in a non-stick frying pan and cook the onion and garlic for 5 mins. Toss the fish pieces with the curry powder and remaining oil. Add to the pan. Cook for another 5 mins, stirring carefully and turning the fish.

2 Add the rice to the pan and turn up the heat, then stir well (the fish will break up a little). Cook for 1–2 mins, then stir in the lemon and parsley. Turn the heat down as low as it will go and put on a lid.

3 Bring a pan of water to the boil, turn down the heat and poach the eggs. Season the kedgeree and divide between plates, topping each with a poached egg.

Nutrition per serving
energy 542 kcals, fat 17g, saturates 4g, carbs 63g, sugars 2g, fibre 3g, protein 31g, salt 0.7g

Fish fingers & mushy peas

There's no need to resort to shop-bought when making your own is so easy – use sustainable pollock and add mint and lemon to your peas.

 PREP 15 mins COOK 10 mins   SERVES 4

- 600g skinless white fish fillets, like pollock or hake
- 50g plain flour, seasoned
- 1 large egg, lightly whisked
- 200g fine fresh breadcrumbs
- 2 tbsp vegetable oil
- 400g frozen peas
- knob butter
- zest 1 lemon, then cut into wedges
- small handful mint, finely shredded
- new potatoes, to serve (optional)

1 Slice the fish into 12 fingers, each about 3cm thick. Put the seasoned flour, egg and breadcrumbs into 3 separate shallow bowls. Dust the fish pieces first in the flour, then coat well in the egg, and cover completely in the breadcrumbs. Put on a plate and chill for 15 mins if you have time.

2 Heat the oil in a large frying pan. Add the fish fingers and fry for 8 mins, turning occasionally, until golden and cooked through. Meanwhile, add the peas to a small pan of boiling water. Cook for 4 mins until tender. Drain, tip into a bowl with the butter, zest and mint, and roughly mash with a potato masher. Season to taste and keep the mushy peas warm.

3 Serve the golden fish fingers with a generous spoonful of peas, lemon wedges and new potatoes, if you like.

Nutrition per serving
energy 489 kcals, fat 11g, saturates 2g, carbs 55g, sugars 5g, fibre 9g, protein 42g, salt 1.3g

Chapter 4

OILY FISH

· ·

Many recognise oily fish for its abundance of healthy omega-3 fatty acids, however several types of oily fish, such as salmon, mackerel and sardines, also offer protein, selenium and B vitamins. Find mouthwatering ways to achieve your omega-3 goals with our quick recipes for pastas, tacos and grills.

Tuna pasta with rocket & parsley pesto

Whizz up a quick homemade pesto with parsley and lemon juice, then serve spooned through hot pasta with fish, tomatoes and green beans.

 PREP 10 mins COOK 15 mins   SERVES 4

- 400g dried pasta
- 140g frozen fine green bean
- 200g cherry tomatoes, halved
- large pack parsley, roughly chopped
- 100g bag rocket
- 185g can tuna in sunflower oil, drained but reserve the oil
- zest and juice 1 lemon
- 185g can tuna in spring water, drained
- 2 tbsp soured cream or cream cheese

1 Cook the pasta in a large pan of salted boiling water, adding the green beans and cherry tomatoes for the final 3 mins of cooking time. Drain, reserving a mug of cooking water.

2 Whizz the parsley, half the rocket, 3 tbsp of oil from the tuna, the lemon zest and juice, and some seasoning with enough of the reserved water in a food processor to form a spoonable pesto dressing.

3 Tip the pasta and veg back into the pan and add the pesto, both cans of tuna and the soured cream or cream cheese, stirring through until hot. Remove from the heat and toss the rest of the rocket through the pasta.

Nutrition per serving
energy 494 kcals, fat 16g, saturates 2g, carbs 56g, sugars 4g, fibre 2g, protein 31g, salt 0.9g

Pepper-crusted salmon with chickpeas

Add a crunchy twist to a classic salmon recipe to create a simple yet special supper.

 PREP 10 mins COOK 15 mins   SERVES 4

- 4 skinless salmon fillets, about 150g each
- 2 tsp black peppercorns
- 1 tsp paprika
- grated zest and juice 2 limes
- 1 tbsp olive oil

FOR THE CHICKPEAS
- 2 x 400g cans chickpeas
- 3 tbsp olive oil
- 2 garlic cloves, finely chopped
- 150ml vegetable stock
- 130g bag baby spinach

1 Heat the oven to 190C/fan 170C/gas 5. Put the salmon fillets in a shallow ovenproof dish in a single layer. Roughly crush the peppercorns with a pestle and mortar, or tip into a cup and crush with the end of a rolling pin. Mix with the paprika, lime zest and a little sea salt. Brush the salmon lightly with oil, then sprinkle over the pepper mix. Bake for 12–15 mins until the salmon is just cooked.

2 Meanwhile, tip the chickpeas into a colander, rinse well under cold running water, then drain. Heat the oil in a pan, add the garlic, then gently cook for 5 mins without browning. Add the chickpeas and stock, then warm through. Crush the chickpeas lightly with a potato masher, then add the spinach and stir well until the leaves are wilted. Add the lime juice and some salt and pepper, then heat through. Serve with the salmon.

Nutrition per serving
energy 531 kcals, fat 32g, saturates 5g, carbs 23g, sugars 2g, fibre 6g, protein 41g, salt 1.01g

Salmon with new potato & corn salad

A no-fuss fish supper made with healthy yet satisfying ingredients, to help you eat well all week.

 PREP 15 mins COOK 15 mins SERVES 4

- 400g baby new potatoes
- 2 sweetcorn cobs
- 4 skinless salmon fillets
- 2 very large tomatoes, like beefsteak

FOR THE DRESSING

- 2 tbsp red wine vinegar
- 2 tbsp extra virgin olive oil
- 1 shallot, finely chopped
- 1 tbsp capers, finely chopped
- handful basil leaves, finely chopped

1 Cook the potatoes in boiling water until tender, adding the corn for the final 5 mins, then drain and allow to cool a little.

2 For the dressing, mix the vinegar, oil, shallot, capers, basil and some seasoning.

3 Heat a grill to high. Rub a little dressing on the salmon and cook, skinned side down, for 7–8 mins. Slice the tomatoes and place on a serving plate. Slice the potatoes, cut the corn from the cobs and arrange over the tomatoes. Top with the salmon, then drizzle over the remaining dressing.

Nutrition per serving
energy 434 kcals, fat 24g, saturates 4g, carbs 28g, sugars 5g, fibre 3g, protein 30g, salt 0.42g

Salmon tacos with chipotle lime yogurt

Grill healthy fish with chipotle spice then serve with cabbage salad, coriander and chilli in soft tortillas.

 PREP 15 mins COOK 10 mins   SERVES 4

- 1 tsp garlic salt
- 2 tbsp smoked paprika
- good pinch sugar
- 500g salmon fillet
- 200ml fat-free yogurt
- 1 tbsp chipotle paste or hot chilli sauce
- juice 1 lime

TO SERVE

- 8 small soft flour tortillas, warmed
- ¼ small green cabbage, finely shredded
- small bunch coriander, picked into sprigs
- few pickled jalapeno chillies, sliced
- lime wedges, to serve
- hot chilli sauce to serve, (optional)

1 Rub the garlic salt, paprika, sugar and some seasoning into the flesh of the salmon fillet. Heat grill to high.

2 Mix the yogurt, chipotle paste or hot sauce and lime juice together in a bowl with some seasoning and set aside. Place the salmon on a baking tray lined with foil and grill, skin-side down, for 7–8 mins until cooked through. Remove from the grill and carefully peel off and discard the skin.

3 Flake the salmon into large chunks and serve with the warmed tortillas, chipotle yogurt, shredded cabbage, coriander, jalapeños and lime wedges. Add a shake of hot sauce, if you like it spicy.

Nutrition per serving
energy 297 kcals, fat 15g, saturates 3g, carbs 8g, sugars 7g, fibre 5g, protein 33g, salt 1.5g

Sushi-style salmon & avocado rice

This dish is a home-style way of serving sushi. Make sure you buy very fresh, sushi-grade salmon and partner with ripe avocados.

 PREP 15 mins COOK 15 mins SERVES 4

- 300g sushi rice
- 350g skinless sushi-grade salmon fillet
- 2 small, ripe avocados, sliced
- juice 1 lemon
- 4 tsp light soy sauce
- 4 tsp toasted sesame seeds
- 2 spring onions, thinly sliced
- 1 red chilli, deseeded and thinly sliced
- small handful coriander leaves

1 Rinse the rice in a sieve until the water runs clear. Drain and put in a large pan with 400ml water. Bring to the boil, turn the heat to low, cover, then cook for 10–12 mins until the rice is almost cooked. Remove from the heat, then leave, covered, for another 10 mins.

2 Thinly slice the salmon and arrange on a platter with the sliced avocado. Drizzle over the lemon juice and soy, making sure everything is evenly covered. Leave in the fridge to marinate for 10 mins.

3 Carefully tip the juices from the salmon platter into the rice, then stir in with a little salt. Divide the rice between 4 bowls. Scatter the sesame seeds, spring onions, chilli and coriander over the salmon and avocado, then serve with the rice.

Nutrition per serving
energy 519 kcals, fat 22g, saturates 3g, carbs 59g, sugars 1g, fibre 2g, protein 25g, salt 1.02g

Tuna, asparagus & white bean salad

A nourishing spring salad, ready in minutes.

PREP 10 mins COOK 5 mins   SERVES 4

- 1 large bunch asparagus
- 2 x cans tuna steaks in water, drained
- 2 x cans cannellini beans in water, drained
- 1 red onion, very finely chopped
- 2 tbsp capers
- 1 tbsp olive oil
- 1 tbsp red wine vinegar
- 2 tbsp tarragon, finely chopped

1 Cook the asparagus in a large pan of boiling water for 4–5 mins until tender. Drain well, cool under running water, then cut into finger-length pieces. Toss together the tuna, beans, onion, capers and asparagus in a large serving bowl.

2 Mix the oil, vinegar and tarragon together, then pour over the salad. Chill until ready to serve.

Nutrition per serving
energy 275 kcals, fat 5g, saturates 1g, carbs 26g, sugars 6g, fibre 8g, protein 33g, salt 1.28g

Mackerel with orange & chilli salad

Packed with omega-3 and vitamin C, this salad couldn't get much healthier –
or tastier.

 PREP 25 mins COOK 5 mins SERVES 4

- 1 tsp black peppercorns
- 1 tsp coriander seeds
- 3 oranges
- 1 red chilli, deseeded,
  finely chopped
- 4 fresh mackerel fillets
- 1 tsp wholegrain mustard
- 1 tbsp clear honey
- 120g bag watercress, spinach
  and rocket salad mix
- 1 shallot, thinly sliced

1 Finely crush the peppercorns and coriander seeds together using a pestle and mortar. Grate the zest from half an orange and mix into the pepper mixture with half the chopped chilli. Lightly slash the skin of the mackerel and press the zesty, peppery mixture onto the fish. Heat the grill.

2 For the salad, segment the oranges. First slice the top and bottom off each orange, then cut away the peel and any white pith using a small, sharp knife. Holding each orange over a bowl to catch all the juice, cut down either side of each segment to release it, then squeeze the shells to release any extra juice. Add 4 tbsp of this juice into a bowl and mix with the mustard, honey and remaining chilli.

3 Grill the mackerel, skin-side up, for 4 mins or until crisp and cooked through. Meanwhile, divide the salad leaves between 4 plates and scatter with the orange segments and sliced shallot. Drizzle with the chilli orange dressing and top with the grilled mackerel.

Nutrition per serving
energy 281 kcals, fat 18g, saturates 4g, carbs 12g, sugars 12g, fibre 2g, protein 17g, salt 0.43g

Hot-smoked trout & mustard salad

A super healthy main meal salad that requires no chopping – just the thing for a busy weeknight.

 PREP 10 mins COOK 5 mins SERVES 4

- 200g green beans, trimmed
- 1 head romaine lettuce, leaves separated and torn if large
- 250g hot-smoked trout
- 50g ready-made croûtons
- 3 tbsp olive oil
- 1 tbsp wholegrain mustard
- zest and juice 1 lemon

1 Cook the green beans in a small pan of boiling salted water for 3–4 mins, until just tender. Drain and refresh under cold running water. Transfer to a serving bowl, add the lettuce, trout and croutons.

2 Whisk the oil with the mustard and lemon zest and juice. Season and drizzle over the salad. Gently toss to coat and serve straight away.

Nutrition per serving
energy 265 kcals, fat 16g, saturates 3g, carbs 12g, sugars 3g, fibre 3g, protein 18g, salt 1.36g

Chapter 5

SHELLFISH

Shellfish are low in calories, while offering a rich source of protein and omega-3 fatty acids. They're also incredibly nutrient dense, supplying a range of micronutrients, such as iron, magnesium, zinc and B12. While shellfish come in all sizes and varieties, here we share our best quick and healthy recipes for smoky spaghetti, fried rice and more.

Spaghetti with smoky seafood sauce

Chilli, fennel seeds and smoked paprika add warmth and flavour to a rich tomato sauce, served with seafood in this quick pasta dish.

 PREP 5 mins COOK 15 mins SERVES 4

- 4 tbsp olive oil
- 4 garlic cloves, crushed
- 1 red chilli, deseeded and finely sliced
- 1½ tsp fennel seeds
- 400g spaghetti
- 2 tsp smoked paprika
- 2 x 400g cans chopped tomatoes
- 2 tsp sugar
- 400g pack frozen mixed cooked seafood, defrosted
- small bunch parsley or basil, chopped

1 Boil the kettle and heat the oil in a large, deep frying pan. Add the garlic, chilli and fennel seeds, and sizzle for a few mins. Pour the boiling water into a large pan and cook the pasta following the packet instructions.

2 Add the paprika, tomatoes, sugar and seasoning to the pan and simmer for 8–10 mins while the pasta cooks.

3 Drain the pasta 1 min before the end of the cooking time, reserving a cup of the water. Add the pasta to the sauce with the seafood. Simmer for 1–2 mins, adding a splash of the reserved pasta water if it looks too thick. Toss the pasta through the sauce as it cooks. Add the herbs and black pepper, then serve.

Nutrition per serving
energy 638 kcals, fat 19g, saturates 3g, carbs 80g, sugars 11g, fibre 7g, protein 35g, salt 0.7g

Fish burgers with spicy mayo

• •

These prawn and salmon burgers are not only fabulously tasty, but they're also healthy too, being rich in omega-3. Make them for the family in just 25 minutes.

 PREP 15 mins COOK 10 mins   SERVES 4

- 180g peeled raw prawns, roughly chopped
- 4 skinless salmon fillets, chopped into small chunks
- 3 spring onions, roughly chopped
- zest and juice 1 lemon
- small pack coriander
- 60g mayonnaise or Greek yogurt
- 4 tsp chilli sauce (we used sriracha)
- 2 Little Gem lettuces, shredded
- 1 cucumber, peeled into ribbons
- 1 tbsp olive oil
- 4 seeded burger buns, toasted, to serve

1 Briefly blitz half the prawns, half the salmon, the spring onions, lemon zest and half the coriander in a food processor until it forms a coarse paste. Tip into a bowl, stir in the rest of the prawns and salmon, season well and shape into 4 burgers. Chill for 10 mins.

2 Mix the mayo and chilli sauce together in a small bowl, season and add some lemon juice to taste. Mix the lettuce with the cucumber, dress with a little of the remaining lemon juice and 1 tsp olive oil, then set aside.

3 Heat the remaining oil in a large frying pan and fry the burgers for 3–4 mins each side or until they have a nice crust and the fish is cooked through. Serve with the salad on the side or in toasted burger buns, if you like, with a good dollop of the spicy mayo.

• •

Nutrition per serving
energy 504 kcals, fat 36g, saturates 5g, carbs 4g, sugars 4g, fibre 3g, protein 39g, salt 0.7g

Prawn fried rice

Make this easy dish in just 30 minutes. It's healthy and low in calories but big on flavour, making it perfect for a speedy family supper.

 PREP 5 mins COOK 25 mins SERVES 4

- 250g long grain brown rice
- 150g frozen peas
- 100g mangetout
- 1½ tbsp rapeseed oil
- 1 onion, finely chopped
- 2 garlic cloves, crushed
- thumb-sized piece ginger, finely grated
- 150g raw king prawns
- 3 medium eggs, beaten
- 2 tsp sesame seeds
- 1 tbsp low-salt soy sauce
- ½ tbsp rice or white wine vinegar
- 4 spring onions, trimmed and sliced

1 Cook the rice following packet instructions. Boil a separate pan of water and blanch the peas and mangetout for 1 min, then drain and set aside with the rice.

2 Meanwhile, heat the oil in a large non-stick frying pan or wok over a medium heat and fry the onion for 10 mins or until golden brown. Add the garlic and ginger and fry for a further minute. Tip in the blanched vegetables and fry for 5 mins, then the prawns and fry for a further 2 mins. Stir the rice into the pan then push everything to one side.

3 Pour the beaten eggs into the empty side of the pan and stir to scramble them. Fold everything together with the sesame seeds, soy and vinegar, then finish with the spring onions scattered over.

Nutrition per serving
energy 418 kcals, fat 11g, saturates 2g, carbs 54g, sugars 7g, fibre 6g, protein 22g, salt 0.5g

Super healthy Singapore noodles

These noodles have it all – healthy, flavour-packed and quick to make, they're sure to be a midweek staple.

 PREP 20 mins COOK 10 mins   SERVES 4

- 3 nests medium egg noodles
- 2 tbsp sunflower oil
- 100g tenderstem broccoli, stems sliced at an angle
- 1 red pepper, deseeded, quartered then cut into strips
- 85g baby corn, quartered lengthways
- 2 garlic cloves, shredded
- 1 red chilli, deseeded and chopped
- thumb-sized piece fresh ginger, peeled and finely chopped
- 2 skinless chicken breasts, sliced
- 100g peeled raw king prawns
- 1 heaped tbsp Madras curry paste
- 2 tsp soy sauce
- 100g beansprouts
- 15g pack coriander, chopped
- 4 spring onions, shredded
- lime wedges, for squeezing

1 Pour boiling water over the noodles and leave to soften. Meanwhile, heat half the oil in a large non-stick wok and stir-fry all the vegetables, except the beansprouts and spring onions, with the garlic, chilli and ginger until softened. If the broccoli won't soften, add a splash of water to the wok and cover to create some steam.

2 Tip the veg on to a plate, add the rest of the oil to the wok, then briefly stir-fry the chicken and prawns until just cooked. Set aside with the vegetables and add the curry paste to the pan. Stir-fry for a few secs then add 150ml water and the soy sauce. Allow to bubble, then add the drained, softened noodles and beansprouts, and toss together to coat.

3 Return the vegetables, chicken and prawns to the wok with the coriander and spring onions. Toss well over the heat and serve with lime wedges.

Nutrition per serving
energy 362 kcals, fat 9g, saturates 1g, carbs 33g, sugars 5g, fibre 6g, protein 40g, salt 1.39g

Crab linguine with chilli & parsley

Keep it simple with this restaurant-style dish that takes a few good-quality ingredients and lets them shine.

 PREP 15 mins COOK 15 mins   SERVES 4

- 400g linguine
- 4 tbsp extra virgin olive oil
- 1 red chilli, deseeded and chopped
- 2 garlic cloves, finely chopped
- small splash, about 5 tbsp, white wine
- 1 whole cooked crab, picked, or about 100g brown crabmeat and 200g fresh white crabmeat
- large handful flat-leaf parsley leaves, very finely chopped
- small squeeze lemon (optional)

1 Bring a large pan of salted water to the boil and add the linguine. Give it a good stir and boil for 1 min less than the packet says.

2 While the pasta cooks, gently heat 3 tbsp of olive oil with the chilli and garlic in a pan large enough to hold all the pasta. Cook the chilli and garlic very gently until they start to sizzle, then turn up the heat and add the white wine. Simmer everything until the wine and olive oil come together.

3 Take off the heat and add the brown crabmeat, using a wooden spoon to mash it into the olive oil to make a thick sauce.

4 When the pasta is ready, turn off the heat. Place the sauce on a very low heat and use tongs to lift the pasta into the sauce.

5 Off the heat, add the white crabmeat and parsley with a sprinkling of sea salt. Stir everything together really well, adding a drop of pasta water if it's starting to get claggy. Season to taste and, if you like, add a small squeeze of lemon. Drizzle with 1 tbsp of oil.

Nutrition per serving
energy 546 kcals, fat 17g, saturates 2g, carbs 74g, sugars 4g, fibre 3g, protein 27g, salt 1.06g

Seafood tagine

Use a frozen mix of fish and shellfish to make this delicious stew, served over a zesty almond couscous.

 PREP 5 mins COOK 15 mins   SERVES 4

- 1 tbsp vegetable oil
- 1 onion, chopped
- 1 red pepper, deseeded and chopped
- 1 garlic clove, finely chopped
- 2 tbsp harissa paste
- 2 x 400g cans chopped tomatoes
- 400g can chickpeas
- 350g pack frozen mixed cooked seafood, defrosted
- 300g couscous
- small pack coriander, leaves only, roughly chopped
- 25g toasted flaked almonds
- zest and juice ½ lemon, reserving the other ½ to serve

1 Heat the oil in a large pan and cook the onion and red pepper for about 5 mins until softened. Stir in the garlic, harissa, chopped tomatoes and chickpeas and cook for about 10 mins until thickened. Add the frozen seafood and cook through for about 10 mins more.

2 Put the couscous in a serving bowl, pour over boiling water to cover, then cover with cling film. Leave to soak while the tagine cooks, then stir in most of the coriander, the almonds, lemon zest and juice, and seasoning. Serve the tagine with the couscous and cut the remaining lemon half into wedges to squeeze over. Sprinkle over the remaining coriander and serve.

Nutrition per serving
energy 564 kcals, fat 11g, saturates 1g, carbs 75g, sugars 13g, fibre 10g, protein 35g, salt 1.47g

Rich paprika seafood bowl

Eating healthy isn't all about salad, this fish stew counts as 3 of your 5-a-day and it's low-fat.

 PREP 5 mins COOK 25 mins   SERVES 4

- 2 tbsp olive oil
- 2 onions, halved and thinly sliced
- 2 celery stalks, finely chopped
- large bunch flat-leaf parsley, leaves and stalks separated
- 2-3 tsp paprika
- 200g roasted red peppers, drained weight, thickly sliced
- 400g can chopped tomatoes with garlic
- 400g white fish fillets, cut into very large chunks
- few fresh mussels

1 Heat 1 tbsp oil in a pan, then add the onions, celery and a little salt. Cover, then gently fry until soft, about 10 mins. Put the parsley stalks, half the leaves, the remaining oil and seasoning into a food processor and whizz to a paste. Add this and the paprika to the softened onions, frying for a few mins. Tip in the peppers and tomatoes with a splash of water, then simmer for 10 mins until the sauce has reduced.

2 Lay the fish and mussels on top of the sauce, put a lid on, then simmer for 5 mins until the fish is just flaking and the mussels have opened – discard any that stay shut. Gently stir the seafood into the sauce, season, then serve in bowls.

Nutrition per serving
energy 200 kcals, fat 7g, saturates 1g, carbs 11g, sugars 8g, fibre 5g, protein 21g, salt 0.3g

Rice & prawn one-pot

A fast and easy meal filled with Mediterranean holiday flavours.

 PREP 5 mins COOK 20 mins SERVES 4

- 1 onion, sliced
- 1 red and 1 green pepper, deseeded and sliced
- 50g chorizo, sliced
- 2 garlic cloves, crushed
- 1 tbsp olive oil
- 250g easy cook basmati rice
- 400g can chopped tomatoes
- 200g peeled raw prawns, defrosted if frozen

1 Boil the kettle. In a non-stick frying or shallow pan with a lid, fry the onion, peppers, chorizo and garlic in the oil over a high heat for 3 mins. Stir in the rice and chopped tomatoes with 500ml boiling water, cover, then cook over a high heat for 12 mins.

2 Uncover, then stir – the rice should be almost tender. Stir in the prawns, with a splash more water if the rice is looking dry, then cook for another min until the prawns are just pink and the rice tender.

Nutrition per serving
energy 365 kcals, fat 7g, saturates 2g, carbs 59g, sugars 7g, fibre 4g, protein 19g, salt 0.85g

Easiest ever seafood rice

Using pre-prepared mixed seafood instantly makes this dish very easy. If you don't eat meat, leave out the chorizo and use fish stock.

 PREP 5 mins COOK 25 mins SERVES 4

- 1 tbsp olive oil
- 1 leek or onion, sliced
- 110g chorizo sausage, chopped
- 1 tsp turmeric
- 300g long grain rice
- 1 litre hot fish or chicken stock
- 200g frozen pea
- 400g pack frozen mixed cooked seafood, defrosted

1 Heat the oil in a deep frying pan, then soften the leek for 5 mins without browning. Add the chorizo and fry until it releases its oils. Stir in the turmeric and rice until coated by the oils, then pour in the stock. Bring to the boil, then simmer for 15 mins, stirring occasionally.

2 Tip in the peas and cook for 5 mins, then stir in the seafood to heat through for a final 1–2 mins cooking or until the rice is cooked. Check for seasoning and serve immediately with lemon wedges.

Nutrition per serving
energy 518 kcals, fat 12g, saturates 0.4g, carbs 75g, sugars 5g, fibre 5g, protein 32g, salt 1.29g

Poor man's vongole rosso

A brilliantly healthy pasta dish that's low calorie and rich in iron too, using budget-friendly cockles instead of clams.

 PREP 5 mins COOK 25 mins   SERVES 4

- 2 tbsp olive oil
- 3 garlic cloves, thinly sliced
- 400g can cherry tomatoes
- glass of white wine
- small pinch golden caster sugar
- 750g cockles, rinsed
- 400g linguine
- 1 tbsp good-quality extra virgin olive oil

1 Heat the olive oil in a large saucepan with a lid. Add the garlic and sizzle for 1 min, then tip in the tomatoes. Use the white wine to swirl round and rinse out the tomato can, then tip it into the pan, sprinkle over the sugar and turn up the heat. Simmer until everything becomes thick, making sure you stir occasionally so it doesn't burn on the bottom of the pan – this will take 15–20 mins.

2 Once the tomatoes have had about 10 mins, cook the pasta in a big pan of salted water until just cooked – this will take about 10 mins – then drain. When the tomatoes and wine have reduced to a thick sauce, throw the cockles into the pan, stir once, cover with a lid and turn the heat up to max. Cook for 3–4 mins until all the cockles have opened, then stir again. Turn off the heat and stir through the pasta with the extra virgin olive oil until everything is coated. Try a strand of pasta and season with salt to taste. Bring the pan to the table with a separate bowl for the shells; serving straight from the pan.

Nutrition per serving
energy 448 kcals, fat 12g, saturates 2g, carbs 59g, sugars 7g, fibre 4g, protein 19g, salt 0.7g

Chapter 6

VEGETARIAN

· ·

Delight in our moreish and balanced vegetarian creations, from creamy pastas to speedy noodles, rice and our best-ever baked eggs – you won't even notice that they're meat-free and they are bursting with goodness!

Tomato, kale, ricotta & pesto pasta

Fresh basil sauce and cherry tomatoes give this healthy dish a beautiful colour – it's also full of fibre and vitamin C.

 PREP 10 mins COOK 15 mins SERVES 4

- 2 tbsp olive oil
- 3 garlic cloves, chopped
- 1 tsp crushed chilli flakes
- 2 x 400g cans cherry tomatoes
- 500g penne
- 200g kale, chopped
- 4 tbsp ricotta
- 4 tbsp fresh pesto
- Parmesan or vegetarian alternative, to serve (optional)

1 Heat the oil in a large saucepan, add the garlic and cook for 2 mins until golden. Add the chilli flakes and tomatoes, season well, and simmer for 15 mins until the sauce is thick and reduced.

2 While the sauce is cooking, cook the pasta following the packet instructions – add the kale for the final 2 mins of cooking. Drain well and stir into the sauce, then divide between 4 bowls. Top each with a dollop of ricotta, a drizzle of pesto and shavings of Parmesan, if you like.

Nutrition per serving
energy 641 kcals, fat 17g, saturates 2g, carbs 99g, sugars 9g, fibre 7g, protein 24g, salt 0.4g

Roast pepper pesto with pasta

This easy pasta dish uses mostly storecupbard ingredients and is ready in minutes. You can buy the roasted garlic purée online or roast your own cloves.

 PREP 10 mins COOK 15 mins SERVES 4

- 2 tbsp roasted garlic purée (or 6 roasted garlic cloves, peeled)
- 450g jar roasted red peppers, drained
- 1 tsp cayenne pepper
- 75g blanched almonds, roughly chopped
- 50g Parmesan or vegetarian alternative, roughly chopped, plus extra for serving (optional)
- 2 tbsp olive oil
- 400g pasta (we used tripolini)
- large pack basil leaves

1 In the small bowl of a food processor, whizz the garlic purée, roasted peppers, cayenne, almonds, Parmesan and oil until it makes a rough pesto consistency. Taste and season.

2 Bring a pan of water to the boil and cook the pasta following the packet instructions. Drain, reserving a little cooking water. Return the pasta to the pan with the pesto, basil and a little of the cooking water, then heat through. Serve with extra Parmesan, if you like.

Nutrition per serving
energy 636 kcals, fat 23g, saturates 5g, carbs 84g, sugars 13g, fibre 8g, protein 22g, salt 0.3g

Healthy pasta primavera

A healthy spaghetti dish full of broad beans, leeks and asparagus tips. Make the most of spring greens with this vibrant, filling pasta recipe.

 PREP 10 mins COOK 20 mins   SERVES 4

- 75g young broad beans (use frozen if you can't get fresh)
- 200g asparagus tips
- 170g peas (use frozen if you can't get fresh)
- 350g spaghetti or tagliatelle
- 175g baby leeks, trimmed and sliced
- 1 tbsp olive oil, plus extra to serve
- 1 tbsp butter
- 200ml fromage frais or crème fraîche
- handful chopped herbs (we used mint, parsley and chives)
- Parmesan or vegetarian alternative, to serve

1 Bring a pan of salted water to the boil and put a steamer (or colander) over the water. Steam the beans, asparagus and peas until just tender, then set aside. Boil the pasta following the packet instructions.

2 Meanwhile, fry the leeks gently in the oil and butter for 5 mins or until soft. Add the fromage frais to the leeks and very gently warm through, stirring constantly to ensure it doesn't split. Add the herbs and steamed vegetables with a splash of pasta water to loosen.

3 Drain the pasta and stir into the sauce. Adjust the seasoning, then serve scattered with shavings of the cheese and drizzled with a little extra olive oil.

Nutrition per serving
energy 476 kcals, fat 9g, saturates 3g, carbs 74g, sugars 6g, fibre 9g, protein 20g, salt 0.1g

Chilli paneer

• •

Try this twist on chilli con carne, which combines beans and warming spices with Indian cheese. It's also served on quinoa instead of rice for extra protein.

 PREP 10 mins COOK 20 mins   SERVES 4

- 140g paneer, cut into small chunks
- 1 tbsp smoked paprika
- 1 tsp rapeseed oil
- 1 red and 1 green pepper, deseeded and diced
- 4 large garlic cloves, sliced
- 2–3 celery sticks, sliced
- 1 tbsp ground cumin
- ½ tsp chilli flakes (optional)
- 2 x 400g cans plum tomatoes
- 2 x 400g cans red kidney beans, undrained
- 2 tsp vegetable bouillon powder
- 2 tsp dried oregano
- 120g quinoa
- 15g coriander, chopped, plus extra to serve, if you like

1 Toss the paneer with ½ tsp of the paprika. Heat the oil in a large non-stick pan over a medium heat, then fry the paneer, turning until golden. Remove from the pan and set aside on a plate, then add the peppers, garlic and celery, remaining paprika, cumin and chilli flakes, and briefly stir over the heat. Tip in the tomatoes and beans along with their juice, the bouillon powder and oregano. Use a wooden spoon to break up the tomatoes if needed, then leave to simmer, uncovered, for 15 mins until the vegetables are tender, stirring occasionally.

2 Meanwhile, cook the quinoa following the packet instructions, drain and set aside for 10 mins. Stir the coriander and paneer into the beans, and sprinkle over extra coriander just before serving.

• •

Nutrition per serving
energy 446 kcals, fat 13g, saturates 5g, carbs 33g, sugars 6g, fibre 12g, protein 17g, salt 1.3g

Veggie spaghetti puttanesca

Sneak in an extra portion of veg in the form of courgettes in this veggie version of puttanesca. Taking just 30 minutes, it's a low-fat and low-calorie meal.

 PREP 5 mins COOK 25 mins SERVES 4

- 2 tbsp olive oil
- 2 onions, finely chopped
- 320g courgettes, coarsely grated
- 3 large garlic cloves, crushed
- ¼–½ tsp chilli flakes (optional)
- 400g can chopped tomatoes
- 2 tbsp tomato purée
- 1 tsp balsamic vinegar
- 1 tsp vegetable bouillon powder
- 8 Kalamata olives, stoned and halved lengthways
- 2 tbsp capers, drained
- 300g wholemeal spaghetti
- 15g flat-leaf parsley, finely chopped
- 40g Parmesan or vegetarian alternative, finely grated

1 Heat the oil in a large non-stick pan over a medium heat. Add the onions and fry for 5 mins until starting to colour. Add the courgette, garlic and chilli flakes, if using, and cook for a further 3–5 mins until the courgette starts to go very soft.

2 Stir in the tomatoes, a can full of water, the tomato purée, vinegar, bouillon, olives and capers, bring to a gentle simmer and cook, uncovered, for 15 mins.

3 Meanwhile, bring a large pan of salted water to the boil. Cook the spaghetti following the packet instructions, then drain and toss with the sauce and parsley. Will keep chilled for up to 3 days. Reheat portions in the microwave until piping hot, or on the hob, covered, over a medium heat with a splash of water to loosen.

Nutrition per serving
energy 444 kcals, fat 12g, saturates 3g, carbs 60g, sugars 11g, fibre 12g, protein 18g, salt 1.1g

Salsa verde baked eggs

Dunk flatbreads into these salsa verde baked eggs to soak up the lovely juices. Healthy and low in calories, it takes just 15 minutes to make.

 PREP 5 mins COOK 15 mins  SERVES 4

- 5 tbsp olive oil
- 1 tsp smoked paprika
- 1 tsp cumin seeds
- 400g can cherry tomatoes
- 200g fresh cherry tomatoes
- 2 garlic cloves
- 1 small bunch parsley
- 1 small bunch basil
- ½ small bunch mint, leaves picked
- 2 tbsp capers
- 1 tsp Dijon mustard
- 2 tbsp white wine vinegar
- 200g baby spinach, washed
- 4 eggs
- ½ tsp chilli flakes (optional)
- flatbreads, to serve (optional)

1 Drizzle 1 tbsp of the olive oil in a frying pan or skillet and fry the paprika and cumin for 30 seconds over a medium heat. Add the canned tomatoes and fresh tomatoes, bring to the boil, then simmer with a lid on over a medium heat for 5–6 mins until the tomatoes have softened.

2 Meanwhile, put the garlic, most of the parsley, the basil, mint, capers, mustard, white wine vinegar, 4 tbsp oil and 3 tbsp cold water in a mini food processor and blitz to a smooth paste. Season.

3 Stir the spinach into the pan with the tomatoes until wilted (put the lid back on for a few minutes, then stir again to help it wilt). Make 4 dips in the mixture and gently crack an egg into each one. Cover with a lid and cook over a medium heat for 6–8 mins, or until the eggs are just set. Uncover the pan, then drizzle over the herby sauce. Scatter over the reserved parsley and chilli flakes, if using. Serve with flatbreads, if you like.

Nutrition per serving
energy 268 kcals, fat 21g, saturates 4g, carbs 7g, sugars 6g, fibre 3g, protein 12g, salt 0.7g

Cumin-spiced halloumi with corn & slaw

Tuck into a super-healthy veggie dinner that's packed with flavour and freshness. We've topped a creamy, zesty coleslaw with pan-fried golden halloumi slices.

 PREP 10 mins COOK 5 mins   SERVES 4

- zest and juice 1 lime
- 1 tsp rapeseed oil
- 1 tsp thyme leaves
- ¼ tsp turmeric
- ¼ tsp cumin seeds
- 1 tbsp chopped coriander
- 1 garlic clove, finely grated
- 100g halloumi, thinly sliced

FOR THE SLAW
- zest and juice 1 lime
- 3 tbsp bio yogurt
- 3 tbsp chopped coriander
- 1 red chilli, chopped
- 160g corn, cut from 2 fresh cobs
- 1 red pepper, deseeded and chopped
- 100g fine green beans, blanched, trimmed and halved
- 200g cherry tomatoes, halved
- 1 red onion, finely sliced
- 320g cabbage, finely sliced

1 Mix the lime zest and juice with the oil, thyme, turmeric, cumin, coriander and garlic together in a bowl. Add the halloumi and carefully turn it until coated – take care as it breaks easily.

2 To make the slaw, mix the lime juice and zest, yogurt, coriander and chilli together, then stir in the corn, red pepper, beans, tomatoes, onion and cabbage.

3 Heat a large non-stick frying pan or griddle pan and fry the cheese in batches for 1 min each side. Serve the slaw on plates with the halloumi slices on top. If you're cooking for 2 people, serve half of the halloumi and slaw and chill the rest for lunch another day.

Nutrition per serving
energy 214 kcals, fat 9g, saturates 5g, carbs 17g, sugars 14g, fibre 8g, protein 12g, salt 0.8g

Peanut noodles with omelette ribbons

Combine egg noodles with fresh flavours – sweet chilli sauce, garlic and coriander – with some Chinese greens and crunchy carrots thrown into the mix.

 PREP 15 mins COOK 15 mins   SERVES 4

- 250g medium egg noodles
- 2 tsp sesame oil, plus a little extra for drizzling
- 1½ tbsp sunflower oil
- 3 carrots, cut into thin batons
- 2 garlic cloves, finely sliced
- ½ Chinese cabbage, roughly sliced
- 5 spring onions, thinly sliced on the diagonal
- 2 tbsp crunchy peanut butter
- 2 tbsp light soy sauce
- 1 tbsp sweet chilli sauce
- 3 eggs, beaten
- handful coriander, roughly chopped, plus a few sprigs to garnish

1 Cook the noodles following the packet instructions. Drain, reserving 2 tbsp of the cooking water. Toss the noodles in a drizzle of sesame oil and set aside.

2 Meanwhile, heat half the sunflower oil in a wok. Add the carrots and stir-fry until tender. Tip in the garlic, cabbage and half the spring onions, and stir-fry for 1–2 mins until the cabbage begins to wilt. Mix the peanut butter, soy, sesame oil, chilli sauce and reserved cooking water together, then add to the pan. Toss in the noodles and heat until warmed through.

3 Whisk the eggs, chopped coriander and some seasoning in a bowl. Heat the remaining sunflower oil in a non-stick frying pan. Tip in the eggs, stir once, then allow to set on one side. Turn over carefully, using a plate if you need to, and cook the other side until set and golden. Slide out onto a board. Cool for 1 min, then cut into strips. Scatter over the noodles, along with the remaining spring onions and a few coriander sprigs.

Nutrition per serving
energy 453 kcals, fat 20g, saturates 4g, carbs 51g, sugars 10g, fibre 7g, protein 16g, salt 1.3g

Black bean tortilla with salsa

Make this frittata for a quick, easy and healthy lunch option, making the most of store cupboard ingredients and packing in 3 of your 5-a-day.

 PREP 10 mins COOK 20 mins   SERVES 4

FOR THE SALSA
- 400g can chopped tomatoes
- 1 onion, finely chopped
- 1 red chilli, deseeded and finely chopped
- 2 tsp smoked paprika
- 15g coriander, finely chopped
- 6 Kalamata olives, thinly sliced
- juice ½ lemon or lime

FOR THE OMELETTE
- 2 x 400g cans black beans, drained
- 3 garlic cloves, finely grated
- 2 tsp ground cumin
- 2 tsp ground coriander
- 6 large eggs
- 1 tbsp rapeseed oil
- 4 generous handfuls rocket

1 Tip the tomatoes into a pan and stir in the onion, half the chilli and the smoked paprika. Cook over a low heat for 10 mins. Tip three-quarters into a bowl, then stir in 2 tbsp of the coriander and the olives and lemon juice.

2 Meanwhile, heat the grill. Tip the beans into a bowl and stir in the remaining chilli, the garlic, cumin and coriander. Beat in the eggs, then add the reserved quarter of the salsa and the remaining fresh coriander with a little salt to taste. Blitz the mixture a little using a hand blender or mash some of the black beans with a potato masher.

3 Heat a 24cm non-stick pan with the oil. Pour in the bean mixture and leave to cook gently for 5–7 mins until the base is set, then grill for 5 mins. Tip out, cut into 4 wedges and serve with the salsa.

Nutrition per serving
energy 368 kcals, fat 14g, saturates 3g, carbs 28g, sugars 7g, fibre 12g, protein 27g, salt 0.5g

Grilled feta with saucy butter beans

Stuck in a food rut? Grab a can of butter beans, some feta and passata to make this super-speedy and super-tasty supper.

 PREP 5 mins COOK 20 mins   SERVES 4

- 500ml passata
- 2 x 400g cans butter beans, drained and rinsed
- 2 garlic cloves, crushed
- 1 tsp dried oregano, plus a pinch
- 200g spinach
- 2 roasted red peppers, sliced
- zest and juice ½ lemon
- 100g feta, cut into chunks
- ½ tsp olive oil
- 4 small pittas

1 Put a large ovenproof frying pan over a medium-high heat, and tip in the passata, butter beans, garlic, oregano, spinach and peppers. Stir together and cook for 6–8 mins until the sauce is bubbling and the spinach has wilted. Season, then add the lemon juice.

2 Heat the grill to high. Scatter the feta over the sauce, so it's still exposed, drizzle with the olive oil and sprinkle over the lemon zest plus a pinch of oregano, then grind over some black pepper. Grill for 5–8 mins until the feta is golden and crisp at the edges.

3 Meanwhile, toast the pittas under the grill or in the toaster, then serve with the beans and feta.

Nutrition per serving
energy 506 kcals, fat 9g, saturates 4g, carbs 69g, sugars 10g, fibre 18g, protein 28g, salt 1.3g

Sweetcorn fritters with eggs & salsa

Get 4 of your 5-a-day in this healthy brunch dish. This recipe makes 4 servings – save half for another day if you're cooking for 2.

 PREP 10 mins COOK 25 mins   SERVES 4

FOR THE FRITTERS & EGGS
- 1 tsp rapeseed oil
- 1 small red onion, finely chopped
- 1 red pepper, deseeded and finely diced
- 100g wholemeal self-raising flour
- 1 tsp smoked paprika
- 1 tsp ground coriander
- 1 tsp baking powder
- 325g can sweetcorn, drained
- 6 large eggs

FOR THE SALSA
- 1 small red onion, finely chopped
- 4 tomatoes (320g), chopped
- 2 x 400g cans black beans, drained
- zest and juice 1 lime
- 15g coriander, chopped

1 Heat the oven to 200C/180C fan/gas 6 and line a large baking tray with parchment.

2 Heat the oil in a small pan and fry the onion and pepper for 5 mins until soft. Meanwhile, mix the flour, spices and baking powder in a bowl. Add the onion, pepper, corn and 2 of the eggs, then mix together well.

3 Spoon 8 mounds of the mixture onto the baking tray, well spaced apart, then flatten slightly with the back of the spoon. Bake for 20 mins until set and golden.

4 Meanwhile, mix together the salsa ingredients and poach the remaining eggs to your liking. Serve the fritters with the eggs and salsa.

Nutrition per serving
energy 437 kcals, fat 12g, saturates 3g, carbs 46g, sugars 12g, fibre 16g, protein 27g, salt 0.9g

Mushroom & thyme risotto

Using a mixture of quinoa and rice gives a light texture and lovely nutty flavour to this dish.

 PREP 5 mins COOK 25 mins   SERVES 4

- 1 tbsp olive oil
- 350g chestnut mushrooms, sliced
- 100g quinoa
- 1 litre hot vegetable stock
- 175g risotto rice
- handful thyme leaves
- handful grated Parmesan or vegetarian alternative
- 50g bag rocket, to serve

1 Heat the oil in a medium pan, sauté the mushrooms for 2–3 mins, then stir in the quinoa. Keeping the vegetable stock warm in a separate pan on a low heat, add a ladle of the stock and stir until absorbed. Stir in the rice and repeat again with the stock, until all the stock has been used up and the rice and quinoa are tender and cooked.

2 Stir in the thyme leaves, then divide between 4 plates or bowls. Serve topped with grated Parmesan and rocket leaves.

Nutrition per serving
energy 302 kcals, fat 7g, saturates 2g, carbs 51g, sugars 4g, fibre 3g, protein 11g, salt 0.74g

Pineapple fried rice

Add chunks of fresh pineapple to fried rice to transform it into something special.
Serve on its own for a family dinner or with other dishes.

 PREP 10 mins COOK 10 mins SERVES 4

- 1½ tbsp sunflower or
  vegetable oil
- 2 eggs, beaten
- 2 garlic cloves, crushed
- small bunch spring onions,
  chopped
- ½ tsp Chinese five-spice
  powder
- 400g cooked long grain rice
- 85g frozen peas
- 2 tsp sesame oil
- 2 tbsp low-salt soy sauce
- 400g fresh pineapple, roughly
  chopped into chunks (about
  ½ medium pineapple)

1 Heat 1 tbsp oil in a wok. Add the eggs,
swirling them up the sides, to make a thin
omelette. Once cooked through, roll the
omelette onto a chopping board and cut
into ribbons.

2 Heat the remaining oil. Add the garlic, onions
and five-spice. Stir-fry until sizzling, then add
the rice (if using pouches, squeeze them first,
to separate the grains), peas, sesame oil and
soy. Cook over a high heat until the rice is hot,
then stir through the pineapple and the
omelette ribbons.

Nutrition per serving
energy 301 kcals, fat 9g, saturates 2g, carbs 44g, sugars 13g, fibre 4g, protein 9g, salt 0.8

Green minestrone with tortellini

Add tortellini to this green minestrone soup with leeks, spring veg and peas for a filling lunch or supper. It's a healthy, low-calorie choice on cold nights.

 PREP 5 mins COOK 25 mins   SERVES 4

- 2 tbsp olive or rapeseed oil
- 1 onion, chopped
- 1 small leek, chopped
- 1 celery stick, chopped
- 3 garlic cloves, crushed
- 2 bay leaves
- 1 litre good-quality chicken or vegetable stock
- 100g shredded spring veg or cabbage
- 50g frozen peas
- zest 1 lemon
- 250g tortellini

1 Heat the olive or rapeseed oil in a large pan. Add the onion, leek and celery stick. Cook for 8–10 mins until softened, then stir in the garlic and bay leaves. Pour in the chicken or vegetable stock, then cover and simmer for 10 mins. Add the spring veg or cabbage, peas, lemon zest and tortellini (spinach tortellini works well).

2 Cover and cook for another 3 mins, season well and ladle into bowls.

Nutrition per serving
energy 231 kcals, fat 8g, saturates 2g, carbs 21g, sugars 6g, fibre 7g, protein 14g, salt 0.9g

Chickpea & coriander burgers

High in fibre, low in fat and counting as 2 of your 5-a-day, this tasty veggie burger delivers on every level.

 PREP 15 mins COOK 10 mins   SERVES 4

- 400g can chickpeas, drained
- zest 1 lemon, plus juice ½
- 1 tsp ground cumin
- small bunch coriander, chopped
- 1 egg
- 100g fresh breadcrumbs
- 1 red onion, ½ diced, ½ sliced
- 1 tbsp olive oil
- 4 small wholemeal buns
- 1 large tomato, sliced, ½ cucumber, sliced and chilli sauce, to serve

1 In a food processor, whizz the chickpeas, lemon zest, lemon juice, cumin, half the coriander, the egg and some seasoning. Scrape into a bowl and mix with 80g of the breadcrumbs and the diced onions. Form 4 burgers, press the remaining breadcrumbs onto both sides and chill for at least 10 mins.

2 Heat the oil in a frying pan until hot. Fry the burgers for 4 mins each side, keeping the heat on medium so they don't burn. To serve, slice each bun and fill with a slice of tomato, a burger, a few red onion slices, some cucumber slices, a dollop of chilli sauce and the remaining coriander.

Nutrition per serving
energy 344 kcals, fat 8g, saturates 1g, carbs 56g, sugars 6g, fibre 6g, protein 15g, salt 1.3g

Red pepper penne & parsley pesto

Try a new take on pesto and blend red peppers, cashew nuts and parsley, then serve spooned through hot pasta.

 PREP 5 mins COOK 10 mins   SERVES 4

- 400g penne
- 290g roasted red peppers, drained
- large handful flat-leaf parsley, plus a few chopped leaves to garnish
- 75g unsalted cashews
- 1 large garlic clove, roughly chopped
- 2 tbsp extra virgin olive oil
- 50g Parmesan or vegetarian alternative, grated

1 Cook the pasta following the packet instructions. Meanwhile, put the peppers, parsley, nuts, garlic and olive oil in a small food processor or mini chopper, and whizz to a pesto consistency. Season and mix in the Parmesan.

2 Drain the pasta and return to the pan with the pesto. Stir and gently heat for 1 min, then sprinkle with a little more chopped parsley and serve.

Nutrition per serving
energy 495 kcals, fat 21g, saturates 5g, carbs 57g, sugars 2g, fibre 1g, protein 20g, salt 0.3g

Chapter 7

VEGAN

· ·

If you're keen to add a few more healthy plant-based meals to your repertoire, this chapter has you covered. We're sharing some of our favourite colourful, comforting and creative vegan recipes, from noodles to pasta, tostadas and chilli. Many of these recipes supply an abundance of vegetables and use simple storecupboard ingredients – perfect for midweek meals.

Butternut squash & chickpea tagine

Make this tasty vegan tagine that kids will love as much as grown-ups. It's a great way to serve 4 of their 5-a-day and it's freezable.

 PREP 5 mins COOK 25 mins   SERVES 4

- 1 tbsp oil
- 1 red onion, finely chopped
- 2 garlic cloves, crushed
- 1 tsp grated ginger
- ½ tsp ground cumin
- 1 tsp ground coriander
- 1 tsp cinnamon
- ¼ tsp mild chilli powder
- 450g bag frozen butternut squash chunks
- 2 carrots, cut into small dice
- 1 courgette, cut into small dice
- 2 x 400g cans chopped tomatoes
- 1 x 400g can chickpeas, drained
- cooked couscous or rice, to serve

1 Heat the oil in a heavy-based pan, then slowly cook the onions for around 10 mins until starting to caramelise. Stir in the garlic, ginger and spices and cook for a further 2 mins.

2 Add the vegetables and canned tomatoes and bring to a simmer. Put the lid on and simmer for around 15 mins or until all the veg are tender.

3 Stir in the chickpeas, heat through and serve with couscous or rice.

Nutrition per serving
energy 221 kcals, fat 5g, saturates 1g, carbs 29g, sugars 15g, fibre 10g, protein 9g, salt 0.1g

Kale pesto pasta

Whizz up kale, pumpkin seeds, basil and garlic to make this easy kale pesto. It's perfect stirred through wholemeal spaghetti for a healthy vegan meal.

 PREP 10 mins COOK 10 mins  SERVES 4

- 150g kale
- small bunch basil
- 1 small garlic clove
- 3 tbsp pumpkin seeds
- 5 tbsp extra virgin olive oil
- 3 tbsp nutritional yeast
- zest and juice 1 lemon
- 350g wholemeal spaghetti

1 Bring a pan of water to the boil. Cook the kale for 30 secs, drain and transfer to a bowl of ice-cold water for 5 mins. Drain again and pat dry with kitchen paper.

2 Put the basil, garlic, seeds, oil, nutritional yeast, lemon juice and zest and drained kale in a food processor. Blitz until smooth, then season. Loosen with a splash of water if it's too thick.

3 Cook the pasta following the packet instructions, then toss with the pesto.

Nutrition per serving
energy 537 kcals, fat 22g, saturates 3g, carbs 60g, sugars 1g, fibre 13g, protein 18g, salt 0.1g

Sesame & spring onion stir-fried udon

Do something different for dinner, with our vegan noodle, tofu, green bean and spring onion stir-fry. It's quick and healthy, plus it's budget-friendly too.

 PREP 15 mins COOK 15 mins   SERVES 4

- 400g firm tofu
- 1 tbsp cornflour
- ½–1 tsp chilli flakes, to taste
- ¼–½ tsp Szechuan peppercorns, ground, to taste
- 1 tbsp vegetable oil
- bunch spring onions, trimmed and cut into lengths
- 200g green beans, trimmed and cut into lengths
- 400g ready-to-use thick udon noodles
- ½ tbsp sesame oil
- 2 tsp sesame seeds, plus a pinch to serve
- 1 tbsp low-salt soy sauce, plus extra to serve
- 1 tbsp rice vinegar

1 Drain and pat the tofu dry with kitchen paper. Cut into cubes, wrap in more kitchen paper, and place a heavy board over the top. Leave to drain for 15 mins.

2 Mix the cornflour, chilli flakes and ground peppercorns together in a bowl with a pinch of salt, then add the tofu. Toss well to coat.

3 Heat half the oil in a large non-stick frying pan over a high heat and fry the tofu pieces for 5–6 mins until golden all over. Scoop out of the pan and leave to drain on kitchen paper.

4 Add the remaining oil to the pan and stir-fry the spring onions and beans for 3–4 mins until tender and lightly golden. Pour a kettle of boiling water over the noodles in a sieve to loosen. Drain well, then tip into the pan. Fry for a few minutes until piping hot. Add the sesame oil and sesame seeds, and sizzle for a few seconds. Splash in the soy sauce, rice vinegar, then add the tofu. Toss well, then serve in bowls with a pinch of sesame seeds on top and more soy sauce on the side.

Nutrition per serving
energy 356 kcals, fat 13g, saturates 2g, carbs 38g, sugars 4g, fibre 4g, protein 18g, salt 0.7g

Tahini lentils

Quick, easy and packed with healthy veg, this is a great midweek meal for vegans and veggies.

 PREP 10 mins COOK 10 mins   SERVES 4

- 50g tahini
- zest and juice 1 lemon
- 2 tbsp olive oil
- 1 red onion, thinly sliced
- 1 garlic clove, crushed
- 1 yellow pepper, deseeded and thinly sliced
- 200g green beans, trimmed and halved
- 1 courgette, sliced into half moons
- 100g shredded kale
- 250g pack pre-cooked puy lentils

1 In a jug, mix the tahini with the zest and juice of the lemon and 50ml of cold water to make a runny dressing. Season to taste, then set the jug aside.
2 Heat the oil in a wok or large frying pan over a medium-high heat. Add the red onion, along with a pinch of salt, and fry for 2 mins until starting to soften and colour. Add the garlic, pepper, green beans and courgette and fry for 5 min, stirring frequently.
3 Tip in the kale, lentils and the tahini dressing. Keep the pan on the heat for a couple of mins, stirring everything together until the kale is just wilted and the lentils are all coated in the creamy dressing.

Nutrition per serving
energy 293 kcals, fat 14g, saturates 2g, carbs 23g, sugars 7g, fibre 10g, protein 13g, salt 0.7g

Cheat's black dhal

• •

If you're eating gluten-free or dairy-free, try this delicious dhal topped with spicy
cauliflower as a filling dinner or as a smaller side dish.

 PREP 10 mins COOK 20 mins   SERVES 4

- 1 small cauliflower, cut into small florets (retain the leaves)
- 2 tsp cumin seeds
- 2 tsp turmeric
- 3 tbsp rapeseed oil (or melted coconut oil)
- 1 small onion, finely chopped
- 1 tbsp garlic paste
- 1 tbsp ginger paste
- 1 red chilli (deseeded if you don't like it too hot), finely chopped
- small pack coriander, stalks chopped, leaves picked to serve
- 2 x 250g pouches puy lentils
- 400ml can coconut milk
- 2 limes, 1 juiced, 1 cut into wedges to serve

1 Heat the oven to 200C/180C fan/gas 6. Toss the cauliflower, including the leaves, with 1 tsp cumin seeds, 1 tsp turmeric and 1 tbsp oil. Season well, spread out on a baking tray and bake for 15–20 mins or until cooked through and a little charred.

2 Heat 1 tbsp oil in a saucepan over a medium heat and add the remaining spices. Once the cumin seeds begin to pop, add the onion and cook for 5 mins or until softened. Stir in the garlic and ginger paste, chilli, coriander stalks and 1 tbsp olive oil, and sizzle for a few mins until fragrant. Stir in the lentils, coating them in the spices, then add the coconut milk and turn up the heat so it bubbles away. Cook for a few mins until the lentils have absorbed some of the coconut milk, then pour in the lime juice and season.

3 Divide the dhal into four bowls, top with the cauliflower and a scattering of coriander leaves and serve with lime wedges on the side.

• •

Nutrition per serving
energy 457 kcals, fat 25g, saturates 5g, carbs 33g, sugars 6g, fibre 12g, protein 17g, salt 1.3g

Hummus pasta salad

Make your own hummus in this family pasta salad. Dish up for little ones first, then scatter with chilli flakes and crumbled feta for the grown-ups.

 PREP 20 mins COOK 10 mins SERVES 4

- 400g can chickpeas, drained and liquid reserved
- 1 tbsp tahini
- 2 tbsp extra virgin olive oil
- ½ garlic clove
- zest and juice ½ lemon
- 250g short pasta of your choice
- 50g baby spinach, roughly chopped
- 200g cherry tomatoes, halved (we used a mixture of red and yellow)
- ¼ cucumber, quartered lengthways and cut into small triangles
- 75g pitted olives of your choice, roughly chopped

1 Boil the kettle. Tip half the chickpeas into a food processor, add roughly half the reserved liquid from the can (the liquid should come to just below the level of the chickpeas in the blender), the tahini, olive oil, garlic, lemon zest and juice and some seasoning. Blitz until you have a smooth, loose hummus. Check for seasoning.

2 Cook the pasta following the packet instructions. Drain, reserving a mugful of the cooking water, and rinse under cold running water for a few seconds until cool.

3 Toss the cooked pasta, spinach, tomatoes, cucumbers, olives, the rest of the chickpeas and the hummus dressing together in a large bowl until everything is well-coated. Add a splash of the reserved pasta cooking water if the dressing is too thick. Will keep covered and chilled for up to 6 hrs, or in an airtight container in a cool bag for 2 hrs. Add a splash of water to loosen the dressing again before serving.

Nutrition per serving
energy 385 kcals, fat 12g, saturates 2g, carbs 51g, sugars 3g, fibre 9g, protein 13g, salt 0.7g

Spinach falafel & hummus bowl

Make this easy vegan salad bowl, with homemade spinach falafels and hummus served alongside pitta and salad. It's packed with nutrients for a healthy supper.

 PREP 5 mins COOK 25 mins   SERVES 4

- 150g baby spinach
- ½ cucumber, sliced
- 1 red onion, finely sliced
- 4 wholemeal pittas, toasted

FOR THE FALAFEL

- 150g baby spinach
- 400g can chickpeas, drained
- 1 garlic clove, chopped
- 1 tsp ground cumin
- ½ small bunch parsley, finely chopped
- 2 tbsp plain flour
- 1 tbsp olive oil

FOR THE HUMMUS

- 400g can chickpeas, drained
- 40ml olive oil, plus extra to serve
- 1 garlic clove, chopped
- juice 1 lemon, plus extra to serve (optional)
- 2 tbsp tahini

1 Heat the oven to 190C/170C fan/gas 5. Line a baking sheet with parchment. Put all the falafel ingredients, except for the oil, in a food processor and season lightly. Pulse until you have a rough mix.

2 Oil your hands lightly, then take tablespoons of the falafel mix, roll into around 16 balls and put on the baking sheet. Press each one down slightly with the palm of your hand. Brush using the 1 tbsp oil and bake for 20–25 mins until firm and golden, turning halfway through.

3 While the falafel is cooking, make the hummus. Put all of the hummus ingredients into a food processor with 50ml of water and blitz until smooth and silky.

4 Put the spinach, cucumber, red onion and falafel in different sections of each bowl, alongside some hummus, then drizzle with the extra olive oil. Grind over some black pepper. Serve with the pittas on the side and more lemon for squeezing over, if you like.

Nutrition per serving
energy 379 kcals, fat 22g, saturates 3g, carbs 27g, sugars 4g, fibre 10g, protein 14g, salt 0.1g

Orzo & tomato soup

Make our simple, budget-friendly tomato, orzo and chickpea soup in just 30 minutes. This easy vegan family meal is healthy and even low fat.

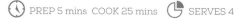 PREP 5 mins COOK 25 mins   SERVES 4

- 2 tbsp olive oil
- 1 onion, chopped
- 2 celery sticks, chopped
- 2 garlic cloves, crushed
- 1 tbsp tomato purée
- 400g can chopped tomatoes
- 400g can chickpeas
- 150g orzo pasta
- 700ml vegetable stock
- 2 tbsp basil pesto
- crusty bread, to serve

1 Heat 1 tbsp olive oil in a large saucepan. Add the onion and celery and fry for 10–15 mins, or until starting to soften, then add the garlic and cook for 1 min more. Stir in all the other ingredients, except for the pesto and remaining oil, and bring to the boil.

2 Reduce the heat and leave to simmer for 6–8 mins, or until the orzo is tender. Season to taste, then ladle into bowls.

3 Stir the remaining oil with the pesto, then drizzle over the soup. Serve with chunks of crusty bread.

Nutrition per serving
energy 349 kcals, fat 12g, saturates 2g, carbs 45g, sugars 9g, fibre 8g, protein 12g, salt 0.6g

Spicy bean tostadas

Tex-Mex goes healthy with these corn tortillas topped with chipotle kidney beans, pickled red onions, coriander and lime.

 PREP 15 mins COOK 15 mins  SERVES 4

- 2 red onions, 1 thinly sliced, 1 finely chopped
- 2 limes, juice of 1 and 1 cut into wedges
- 1½ tbsp sunflower oil
- 2 garlic cloves, finely chopped
- 2 tsp ground cumin
- 1 tbsp tomato purée
- 1 tbsp chipotle paste
- 400g can kidney beans, drained and rinsed
- 4 corn tortillas
- 40g radishes, thinly sliced
- large handful coriander, roughly chopped

1 Heat the oven to 220C/200C fan/gas 7. Put the sliced onion, lime juice and seasoning in a bowl, and set aside.
2 Heat 1 tbsp of the oil in a pan and fry the chopped onion and garlic until tender. Stir in the cumin and fry for 1 min more. Add the tomato purée, chipotle paste and beans, stir, then tip in half a can of water. Simmer for 5 mins, season, then roughly mash to a purée. (You can cook for a few mins more if it is a bit runny or add a few splashes of water to thin.)
3 Meanwhile, brush the tortillas with the remaining oil and place on a baking sheet. Bake for 8 mins until crisp. Spread the tortillas with the bean mixture. Mix the radishes and coriander with the pickled onions, then spoon on top. Serve with lime wedges.

Nutrition per serving
energy 244 kcals, fat 5g, saturates 2g, carbs 34g, sugars 7g, fibre 6g, protein 8g, salt 0.7g

30-minute courgettes with dukkah

Get 4 of your 5-a-day in one vegan dinner! This easy recipe is healthy and gluten-free, and provides calcium, folate, fibre, vitamin C and iron.

 PREP 10 mins COOK 20 mins   SERVES 4

- 1 tbsp rapeseed oil
- 2 onions, halved and sliced
- 2 tsp ground coriander
- 2 tsp smoked paprika
- 400g can chopped tomatoes
- 2 tsp vegetable bouillon powder
- 2 large courgettes, sliced
- 400g can butter beans, drained
- 180g cherry tomatoes
- 160g frozen peas
- 15g coriander, chopped

FOR THE DUKKAH
- 1 tsp coriander seeds
- 1 tsp cumin seeds
- 1 tbsp sesame seeds
- 25g flaked almonds

1 Heat the oil in a large non-stick pan and fry the onions for 5 mins, stirring occasionally until starting to colour. Stir in the ground coriander and paprika, then tip in the tomatoes with a can of water. Add the bouillon powder and courgettes, cover and cook for 6 mins.

2 Meanwhile, make the dukkah. Warm the whole spices, sesame seeds and almonds in a pan until aromatic, stirring frequently, then remove the pan from the heat.

3 Add the butter beans, tomatoes and peas to the courgettes, cover and cook for 5 mins more. Stir in the coriander, then spoon into bowls. Crush the spices, seeds and almonds using a pestle and mortar and scatter on top. If you're cooking for 2 people, put half the seed mix in a jar and chill half the veg for another day.

Nutrition per serving
energy 495 kcals, fat 21g, saturates 5g, carbs 57g, sugars 2g, fibre 1g, protein 20g, salt 0.3g

Five-bean chilli

Batch-cook this vegan five-bean chilli, then freeze in portions for busy weeknights. With beans, tomatoes and peppers, it's full of nutritious, filling veg.

 PREP 5 mins COOK 30 mins   SERVES 4

- 1½ tbsp rapeseed oil
- 1 onion, sliced
- 2 peppers, sliced
- 2 garlic cloves, crushed
- 1 tbsp ground cumin
- 1 tbsp ground coriander
- 2 tsp hot smoked paprika
- 400g can chopped tomatoes
- 400g can mixed beans, drained
- 400g can black beans, drained
- pinch sugar
- 250g brown rice
- ½ small bunch coriander, chopped
- soured cream or guacamole, to serve (optional)

1 Heat the oil in a casserole dish and fry the onion and peppers for 10 mins over a medium heat until the onion is golden brown. Add the garlic and spices, and fry for 1 min. Pour in the tomatoes, both cans of beans, 50ml water, then add the sugar and season. Simmer, stirring regularly, for 15–20 mins until thickened.

2 Meanwhile, cook the rice following the packet instructions. Serve the chilli on the rice and scatter over the coriander. Top with a spoonful of soured cream, or guacamole, if you like.

Nutrition per serving
energy 439 kcals, fat 8g, saturates 1g, carbs 69g, sugars 10g, fibre 14g, protein 16g, salt 0.04g

Index